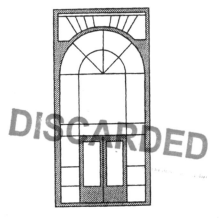

Stranger Than Fiction

A BOOK OF LITERARY LISTS

Stranger Than Fiction

A BOOK OF LITERARY LISTS

Aubrey
Dillon Malone

CB
CONTEMPORARY BOOKS

Cover artwork by Andy Parker
This edition of *Stranger Than Fiction* is published under license from
Prion Books Limited, London.

This edition first published in 2000 by Contemporary Books
A division of NTC/Contemporary Publishing Group, Inc.
4255 West Touhy Avenue, Lincolnwood (Chicago), Illinois
60712-1975 U.S.A.
Printed and bound in Great Britain by Creative Print and Design, Wales
International Standard Book Number: 0-8092-9904-6
22 21 20 19 18 17 16 15 14 13 12 11 10 9 8 7 6 5 4 3 2 1

Subjects A-Z

ABUSE, ACCIDENTS, ACTORS, ACTRESSES, ADVERTISING, ADVANCES,
ADVICE, AFFAIRS, ALCOHOL, ANAGRAMS, ARRESTS,
(CHARACTER) ASSASSINATIONS, AUTO ACCIDENTS

BED, THE BIBLE, BIOPICS, BIRTHPLACES, BOOKS FOR CHANGE, BISEXUALS,
(WRITER'S) BLOCK, BOXERS, BURIAL, BURNING BOOKS

CATS, CHARACTERS, CHILDREN'S BOOKS, CONSTIPATION, COPYRIGHT, CYNICS

DEATH, DEDICATIONS, DETECTIVES, *DOUBLE ENTENDRES*, DROWNINGS

EARLY STARTERS, ECCENTRICS, EDITORS, EDITING, EGOS, EPITAPHS,
EXECUTIONS, EXILES, EXPATRIATES, EYES

FACT AND FICTION, FATHERS, FEUDS, FICTIONAL WORLDS, FILM,
FINANCE, FIRST PAPERBACKS, FIRST NIGHTS, FLAGELLATION, FRIENDSHIPS

GAMBLING, GENDER, GUNS

HEMORRHOIDS, HALLUCINATIONS, HOBBIES, HYPOCHONDRIACS

ILLEGITIMATE CHILDREN, INCEST, INITIALS, INSANITY, INSOMNIA,
INSPIRATION, INSULTS

JAIL, JOURNALISM

KNIGHTHOODS

A

VERBAL ABUSE
10 classics in the claws of the critics

The Outsider
"This book is inaccurate in detail and fraudulent in method to the point of being very bad. The reason these things were not detected by the reviewers is because it said what they wanted to hear."

Martin Green

Waiting for Godot
"Another of those plays that tries to lift superficiality to significance through obscurity. It should please those who prefer to have their clichés masquerade as epigrams."

Milton Shulman

Jude the Obscure
"The village aesthetic brooding over the village idiot."

G. K. Chesterton

Ulysses
"In Ireland they try to make a cat clean by rubbing its nose in its own filth. Mr. Joyce has tried the same treatment on the human subject."

George Bernard Shaw

Finnegans Wake
"Obviously schizophrenia."

Comment of a psychiatrist to Oliver St. John Gogarty
on Joyce's *meisterwork*

On the Road
"That's not writing, it's just typing."

Truman Capote

An Ideal Husband
"So helpless, so crude, so bad, so clumsy, feeble, and vulgar."

Henry James

The Naked and the Dead
"A clever, talented, admirably executed fake."

Gore Vidal

Moby Dick
"Melville knows nothing of the sea."

Joseph Conrad

Our Mutual Friend
"To our perception, the poorest of Mr. Dickens' works. And it is poor with the poverty not of momentary embarrassment, but of permanent exhaustion."

Henry James

SHORT CUTS
30 succinct character assassinations

RALPH WALDO EMERSON
"One of those people who would be enormously improved by death."

Saki

ALGERNON CHARLES SWINBURNE
"Swine Born."

Punch magazine

ARNOLD BENNETT
"The Hitler of the book racket."

Percy Wyndham Lewis

JOSEPH CONRAD
"The wreck of Stevenson floating about in the slip-slop of Henry James."

George Moore

TRUMAN CAPOTE
"A sweetly vicious old lady."

Tennessee Williams

IAN FLEMING
"Someone who got off with women because he couldn't get on with them."

Rosamond Lehmann

ALDOUS HUXLEY
"A stupid person's idea of a clever person."

Elizabeth Bowen

LYTTON STRACHEY
"The arch-bugger of Bloomsbury."

Quentin Bell

THOMAS HARDY
"An abortion of George Eliot."

George Moore

AUBREY BEARDSLEY
"Daubaway Weirdsley."

Linley Sambourne

EZRA POUND
"A sort of revolutionary simpleton."

Percy Wyndham Lewis

J. D. SALINGER
"The greatest mind ever to stay in prep school."

Norman Mailer

GEORGE BERNARD SHAW
"An atheist trembling in the haunted corridor."

W. B. Yeats

SAM SHEPARD
"The mind of a Kafka trapped in the body of a Jimmy Stewart."
Michael Feingold

GERTRUDE STEIN
"A woman masterly in making nothing happen very slowly."
Clifton Fadiman

JAMES THURBER
"A tall, thin spectacled man with the face of a harassed rat."
James Maloney

P. G. WODEHOUSE
"English literature's performing flea."

Sean O'Casey

STEPHEN FRY
"A young man with all the wit of an unflushed toilet."
Bernard Manning

FORD MADOX FORD
"Freud Madox Fraud."

Osbert Sitwell

EDGAR ALLAN POE
"A kind of Hawthorne with delirium tremens."

Leslie Stephen

THOMAS CARLYLE
"The same old sausage, fizzing and sputtering in its own grease."
Henry James

T. E. LAWRENCE
"A man with a genius for backing into the limelight."
Lowell Thomas

ERNEST HEMINGWAY
"A guy who keeps saying things over and over until you believe it must be good."

Raymond Chandler

W. H. AUDEN
"All ice and wooden-faced acrobatics."

Percy Wyndham Lewis

JAMES JOYCE
"An essentially private man who wished his total indifference to public notice to be universally recognized."

Tom Stoppard

DANTE ALIGHIERI
"A hyena that wrote poetry in tombs."

Friedrich Nietzsche

TOM WOLFE
"A pretentious fad-chaser, the pom-pom girl of American letters."

Edward Albee

WILLIAM WORDSWORTH
"A half-witted sheep who bleated articulate monotony."

James Stephens

KATE MILLETT
"An imploding beanbag of poisonous self-pity."

Camille Paglia

VICTOR HUGO
"A madman who believed himself to be Victor Hugo."

Jean Cocteau

DAMAGE

5 writers involved in tragic accidents

WILLIAM S. BURROUGHS
Shot his common-law wife to death accidentally in 1951 when trying to shoot a glass off the top of her head. Spent (or so he said) the rest of his life trying to purge himself for his carelessness through the exorcism of literature.

JOHN DOS PASSOS
Was involved in a horrific auto crash in 1947. Blinded by the sun, he hit a parked truck. His wife Katy was thrown through the windscreen and decapitated. He himself lost an eye.

CHARLES DICKENS
While on a train journey in Kent in 1864 with the half-completed manuscript of *Our Mutual Friend*, the train was derailed and some of the carriages plunged over a bridge. Miraculously he survived, as did his manuscript, but the experience didn't do him much good and afterward he became increasingly agitated when writing anything. Perhaps unsurprisingly, this was the last book that he completed. He died in 1870.

GUSTAVE FLAUBERT
His father spilled boiling water on his hand, when he was a boy, causing partial paralysis and a permanent scar.

STEPHEN KING
In 1999, in a bizarre cross between the plots of his horror novels *Christine* and *Misery,* King suffered a punctured lung, had both his legs and his pelvis broken when he was hit by an out-of-control van that mounted the sidewalk while he was walking near his home in Maine.

CRASH!

5 writers killed in auto accidents

RICHARD FARIÑA
This 1960s one-novel-wonder was killed in a motorbike accident at 28 after a life lived dangerously.

T. E. LAWRENCE
Died of head injuries following a motorcycle accident in Dorset, England, in 1935 when he was 46.

MARGARET MITCHELL
The *Gone with the Wind* author died at the age of 49 after an auto accident in Atlanta.

ALBERT CAMUS
Once said that the most existentially absurd thing that could happen to a person was to die in an auto accident. Ironically, this was how he died in 1960 at the age of 47.

NATHANAEL WEST
Killed in an auto crash with his wife just two days after they were married. He was 37.

AMATEUR DRAMATICS

5 novelists who were also actors

Yukio Mishima
Wilkie Collins
Charles Dickens
Albert Camus
George Grossmith

AN IDEAL HUSBAND
15 writers who married actresses

Malcolm Lowry (Margerie Bonner)
Erich Maria Remarque (Paulette Goddard)
Philip Roth (Claire Bloom)
Roald Dahl (Patricia Neal)
Neil Simon (Marsha Mason)
Dion Boucicault (Agnes Robertson)
Sean O'Casey (Eileen Carey)
Anton Chekhov (Olga Knipper)
Bertolt Brecht (Helene Wiegel)
Arthur Miller (Marilyn Monroe)
Sam Shepard (Jessica Lange)
Robert Bolt (Hayley Mills)
John Osborne (Jill Bennett)
Thomas Moore (Bessie Dyke)
J.M. Barrie (Mary Ansell)

AD LIBBERS
5 writers who gave good copy

FAY WELDON
As an advertising copywriter, she devised the famous "Go to work on an egg" campaign.

SALMAN RUSHDIE
Was responsible for coining the phrase "Naughty but nice" for the real-cream TV ads.

ERNEST HEMINGWAY
Appeared in several ads endorsing both Parker pens and
Ballantine ale in the pages of *Life* magazine.

DOROTHY L. SAYERS
During her stint in the advertising world, Sayers coined the
classic "Guinness is good for you" slogan.

BRENDAN BEHAN
Was asked to think of a slogan for Guinness and came up with
this inspirational gem: "It makes you drunk."

FEEDING FRENZY
15 notably generous advances

THOMAS MOORE
Received a 3,000-guinea (£3,150) advance for *Lalla Rookh* in
1817, a record figure for a poet at that time.

FREDERICK FORSYTH
Received £3 million for *The Fourth Protocol*. He was also given
£250,000 for *The Devil's Alternative* purely on the strength of
the synopsis.

TOM WOLFE
Received a $7.5-million advance for *A Man in Full*. The 742-
page novel that took him eleven years to write. It had a 1.2-million
first print run, a $500,000 marketing budget, and *Rolling Stone*
magazine paid a record $600,000 for the serial rights.

E. L. DOCTOROW
Was given an advance of $1.3 million for his masterpiece
Ragtime in 1976.

MARILYN FRENCH
Received a $1.9-million advance for *The Bleeding Heart* in 1979, after the success of *The Women's Room* two years earlier.

JUDITH KRANTZ
Bantam paid her nearly $3.5 million for *Princess Daisy* in 1979, with Corgi offering a further £450,000 for the British rights.

COLLEEN MCCULLOUGH
Received $1.9 million for the paperback rights to *The Thorn Birds* in 1978.

SIR WALTER SCOTT
Was offered a £1,000 advance for *Marmion* by Constable before they had read a line.

MARTIN AMIS
Received a £500,000 advance for *The Information* after switching agents from Pat Kavanagh to Andrew "the Jackal" Wylie.

JAMES CLAVELL
Got $5 million for *Whirlwind* from William Morrow & Co in 1986.

BARBARA TAYLOR BRADFORD
Received a $27-million advance from HarperCollins in 1992 for her next three novels.

STEPHEN KING
Offered an advance of $40 million for a three-book deal in 1989.

TOM CLANCY
Received $22 million from Berkeley Putnam for the North American rights to *Without Remorse* in 1992. In 1997, he was given $75 million for a two-book deal with Penguin.

MONICA LEWINSKY
In March 1999, St. Martin's Press offered $600,000 for her kiss-and-tell tome *Monica's Story* chronicling her fling with Bill Clinton.

NICK HORNBY
Received a £2-million two-book advance from Penguin in 1998.

GRUB STREET

5 not-so-generous advances

EDGAR ALLAN POE
Offered a mere $14 for *Eureka* towards the end of his life – and this with the proviso that if the book didn't earn that amount, he had to make up the difference to the publisher.

JOHN CLELAND
Received just 20 guineas for *Fanny Hill* from a London publisher in 1749. The pioneering erotic novel went on to be translated into several European languages and netted the aforementioned opportunist over £10,000: a not-inconsiderable sum at the time.

THOMAS WOLFE
Received only $500 for his massive work *Look Homeward, Angel* … which worked out at about a penny for every hundred words.

JACK LONDON
Got a $2,000 flat fee for *The Call of the Wild* in 1903. The book sold so well he lost at least of $100,000 by giving up the royalties.

ERNEST HEMINGWAY
Settled for no advance at all—just a handshake from Paris publisher Robert McAlmon—for his first collection *Three Stories and Ten Poems*. He was happy just to get it published.

CURTAIN CALLS
10 pieces of advice for aspiring playwrights

"Very few plays are any good, and NO first plays are any good."
George Abbot

"The first rule for any young playwright to follow is not to write like Henry Arthur Jones. The second and third rules are the same."
Oscar Wilde

"One begins with two people on a stage, and one of them had better say something pretty damn quick."
Moss Hart

"The most important ingredients of a play are life, death, food, sex, and money—but not necessarily in that order."
Noel Coward

"Plays are not written; they're rewritten."
Dion Boucicault

"Writing a play is the most difficult thing a writer can do with a pen."
Kenneth Tynan

"Depending upon shock tactics is easy, whereas writing a good play is difficult. Pubic hair is no substitute for wit."
J. B. Priestley

"What should the theater be? The theater should be full."
Giuseppe Verdi

"A first-night audience consists of the unburied dead."

Orson Bean

"A plagiarist is a writer of plays."

Oscar Wilde

THE WRITE STUFF

10 pieces of advice for aspiring writers

"Read over your compositions, and when you meet a passage which you think is particularly fine, strike it out."

Samuel Johnson

"Write without pay until somebody offers it. If nobody does so within three years, sawing wood is what you were intended for."

Mark Twain

"The most essential gift for a good writer is a built-in shock-proof shit detector."

Ernest Hemingway

"Don't make classical quotations. That's like digging up your grandmother in front of your mistress."

Leon-Paul Fargue

"If you read twenty or thirty pages by a writer and want to continue, you are swimming in his sea. He can write quite badly after that because you're hooked."

Brian Moore

"The principle of writing is to make your mother and father drop dead of shame."

J. P. Donleavy

"No one can ever write about anything that happened to him after he was 12 years old."

Ignazio Silone

"There are three basic rules for writing a novel. Unfortunately, nobody knows what they are."

W. Somerset Maugham

"Writing is easy. All you do is sit staring at a blank sheet of paper until the drops of blood form on your forehead."

Gene Fowler

"If you are a writer, there will come at least one morning in your life when you wake up and want to kill your agent."

Bernice Rubens

THE LANGUAGE OF LOVE
10 literary affairs

H. G. WELLS AND REBECCA WEST
They met after West had rubbished Wells's book *Marriage* in a review. He repaid her unkindness by falling in love with her. She was twenty-five years younger than him but their affair lasted ten years. It concluded after another of Wells's lovers, Australian journalist Hedwig Verena Gatternigg, tried to kill herself in his flat after a row with Wells. West's only child was fathered by him.

15

EDMUND WILSON AND EDNA ST. VINCENT MILLAY
Wilson was thoroughly infatuated by poet and noted nymph-
omaniac Millay when they first met, and engaged in a whirlwind
romance with her. It finally foundered due to *wanderlust* on her
part.

JEAN-PAUL SARTRE AND SIMONE DE BEAUVOIR
The two great minds ("It was the first time I'd ever felt intellectually inferior to anyone," de Beauvoir later commented) met at
university in 1929 and formed one of the great literary bondings
of the century. They lived together off and on until Sartre's death
in 1980, the relationship fortified rather than endangered by the
freedom they allowed one another to take other partners.

DASHIELL HAMMETT AND LILLIAN HELLMAN
Met in 1930 when Hammett was a Hollywood screenwriter and
had a passionate affair. They remained friends until Hammett's
death in 1961.

ANAÏS NIN AND HENRY MILLER
Nin met Miller after she published a biography of D. H.
Lawrence in Paris in 1932 and thus began a torrid romance. It
was carried on almost under the eyes of Nin's husband, though
he never suspected a thing. When it ended, she went back to
him, accusing Miller of reducing all women to "an aperture, a
biological sameness."

SEAN O'FAOLÁIN AND ELIZABETH BOWEN
Had an affair while Bowen was married to Alan Cameron.

ELIZABETH SMART AND GEORGE BARKER
The tragic love affair between the married English poet and the
Canadian writer is chronicled in her *By Grand Central Station I
Sat Down and Wept*. She fell in love with his poetry and bore
him four children.

LORD BYRON AND LADY CAROLINE LAMB
After the poet and novelist slept together for the first time they exchanged locks of pubic hair.

NELSON ALGREN AND SIMONE DE BEAUVOIR
They met in 1947 when Algren acted as her guide around Chicago. She painted a loving picture of him in her novel *The Mandarins*. He was rather less generous about her, once saying that "she couldn't write a scene in a restaurant without telling you everything on the menu."

F. SCOTT FITZGERALD AND DOROTHY PARKER
Had a brief affair while he was married to the unstable Zelda. According to Sheilah Graham, it was motivated by compassion on her part and despair on his.

A WALK ON THE WILD SIDE
5 gay and lesbian affairs

VIRGINIA WOOLF AND VITA SACKVILLE-WEST
Though Woolf was married, she was bisexual and carried on a five-year affair with Sackville-West, with whom she fell madly in love after meeting her in 1923. Her husband Leonard knew about their relationship, but said it didn't pose a threat to the stability of their marriage.

W. H. AUDEN AND CHRISTOPHER ISHERWOOD
Longtime friends as well as lovers and literary collaborators. Sex, according to Isherwood, gave their friendship an extra dimension.

ARTHUR RIMBAUD AND PAUL VERLAINE
Began an affair in Paris in 1871, which was punctuated by savage jealousy and violence. When Rimbaud tried to terminate the affair, Verlaine shot and wounded him and was imprisoned for attempted murder.

JOE ORTON AND KENNETH HALLIWELL
Would-be playwright Halliwell became increasingly jealous of Orton's success and promiscuity. He beat him to death with a hammer and took his own life with an overdose in 1967.

CARSON MCCULLERS AND KATHERINE ANNE PORTER
Despite being married twice (to the same man), McCullers had several affairs with other women writers.

IN PRAISE OF OLDER WOMEN
5 writers' affairs with their seniors

RAINER MARIA RILKE
Had a lengthy affair with Lou Andreas-Salomé in the 1890s. She was thirteen years older than him. (Nietzsche also fell in love with her.)

HONORÉ DE BALZAC
Had a steamy affair with Laure de Berny when he was 23, and she was 45 … and a grandmother.

W. SOMERSET MAUGHAM
Seduced by the 41-year-old Violet Hunt when he was 29.

THOMAS WOLFE
On his 25th birthday, he took Aline Bernstein, who was 44, as his mistress.

RAYMOND CHANDLER
His wife Pearl Bowen was seventeen years older than him.

THE BATTLE WITH THE BOTTLE

10 writers on alcohol

"I'm not a writer with a drinking problem. I'm a drinker with a writing problem."

Brendan Behan

"Randall Jarrell is the only poet I ever knew who didn't drink."

John Berryman

"When I have one martini I feel bigger, wiser, taller. When I have a second, I feel superlative. After that, there's no holding me."

William Faulkner

"Drinking makes you loquacious, as we all know, and if what you've got for company is a piece of paper, then you're going to talk to it."

Madison Bell

"Alcohol is like love. The first kiss is magic. The second is intimate, the third, routine. After that you just take the girl's clothes off."

Raymond Chandler

"Some American writers who have known each other for years have never met in the daytime or when both were sober."

James Thurber

"First you take a drink, then the drink takes a drink, then the drink takes you."

F. Scott Fitzgerald

"If a man tells you he has mastered whiskey, you can be sure it's the whiskey that is talking."

John B. Keane

"One reason I don't drink is because I want to know when I'm having a good time."

Nancy Astor

"It costs money to die of cirrhosis of the liver."

P. G. Wodehouse

THROUGH A GLASS DARKLY
10 literary tipplers

ROBERT BENCHLEY
An acquaintance who was worried about his alcohol intake informed him that alcohol was "slow poison." Benchley replied, "So who's in hurry?"

RING LARDNER
Was sitting at the bar counter of a theater nightclub one night when a flamboyant actor with a wild mane of hair walked in. Eyeing him up and down, Lardner said, "Tell me, how do you look when I'm sober?"

LORD BYRON
Once drank burgundy from a human skull.

BRENDAN BEHAN
A fairly typical example: at a dress rehearsal for *The Quare Fellow*, he arrived drunk and proceeded to fall asleep in one of the seats. When he woke up he started hurling abuse at all the actors, with a generous supply of expletives. One of them said to the director, "Will you please throw that man out so we can get on with the work." "I can't," the beleaguered director replied, "he's the author!"

ARTHUR KOESTLER
After a drunken spree with Albert Camus in France in 1941, challenged Camus to a race across the Place St. Michel ... on all fours. (Koestler won, but Camus accused him of standing up before they reached the curb.)

GEOFFREY CHAUCER
Was given a pitcher of wine every day when he was poet laureate, as one of the perks of the post.

EDGAR ALLAN POE
An alcoholic and a laudanum addict, he still managed to join his local Temperance Society to lecture others on the evils of the demon drink.

SAMUEL JOHNSON
Was once reputed to have drunk thirty-six glasses of port during the course of an evening.

R. B. SHERIDAN
Was so fond of the drop that he was even partial to eau de cologne if there was nothing else available. He didn't deny himself his tipple even as the Drury Lane Theatre burned to cinders in front of him in 1809: "A man," he said, smiling through his tears, "must surely be allowed a glass of wine by his own fireside." And who could begrudge him it?

DYLAN THOMAS

When under the influence, he often got on all fours and barked like a dog. He took this to its extreme one day in a hotel, where he pretended he was rabid, chasing the guests around the lobby as he champed at their feet. (The exhibition ended when he finally went outside and chipped one of his teeth on a lamppost.)

IN OTHER WORDS

20 authorial anagrams

GORE VIDAL
Regal Void

STEPHEN KING
Peek 'n' things

T. S. ELIOT
Toilets

DAVID MAMET
I made mad TV

NORMAN MAILER
I'm near normal

SALMAN RUSHDIE
Iran's sham duel

D. H. LAWRENCE
Wencher lad

P. J. O'ROURKE
Pour, joker

MAEVE BINCHY
Ha! Vice by men

GEORGE MOORE
Ergo more ego

ERNEST HEMINGWAY
Write, gene-shy man

RAYMOND CHANDLER
Darned charm only

NICCOLÒ MACHIAVELLI
Me a cool chic villain

DYLAN THOMAS
Hot lady's man

ENID BLYTON
Tiny blonde

WILLIAM SHAKESPEARE
Am I a weakish speller

SAMUEL TAYLOR COLERIDGE
Rue lost ode: a lyrical gem

MARCEL PROUST
Pure calm sort

ROBERT LOUIS STEVENSON
Our best novelist, señor

WILLIAM WORDSWORTH
Wow, small horrid wit

ARRESTED DEVELOPMENTS

5 writers who were arrested

GEOFFREY CHAUCER
Charged with rape in 1380. The matter was settled out of court.

R. B. SHERIDAN
Was drunk and disorderly on the opening night of *A School for Scandal* in 1777.

TRUMAN CAPOTE
Arrested for driving while drunk and having no license in 1983. He appeared in court dressed in shorts and sandals.

OLIVER GOLDSMITH
Arrested in 1766 for not paying his rent, and released only after Dr. Johnson had managed to raise the cash by selling the manuscript of *The Vicar of Wakefield* for £60.

HERMAN MELVILLE
Arrested and briefly jailed in Tahiti as a member of the mutinous crew of an Australian whaling ship.

B

BETWEEN THE COVERS
5 authors who liked to write in bed

ROBERT LOUIS STEVENSON
Coughed so much from his tuberculosis that he was often reduced to writing in bed for long periods.

EDITH WHARTON
Liked working in bed so much that she once threw a tantrum because the bed in her hotel room wasn't facing the light.

MARK TWAIN
Not only did he write in bed, but he even stayed in his pajamas when receiving visitors.

ERNEST HEMINGWAY
Wrote in bed when he was suffering from insomnia.

VOLTAIRE
Often spent sixteen hours a day there, scribbling away.

"THE" BOOK
10 facts about the Bible

A 1631 edition contained the exhortation: "Thou shalt commit adultery." The English monarch of the time, Charles I, was horrified, and he recalled all 1,000 copies, as well as fining the printers £3,000.

The book of Ecclesiastes recommends clearing the stomach by throwing up before or during a meal to make way for more food.

The word "girl" appears only once in the whole book.

In 1272, a copy in nine handwritten volumes cost £33.

In one of Paul's letters to the Corinthians, he writes: "Once I was stoned." That has now been changed to "Once I received a stoning."

The Bible isn't renowned for its humor, but in Job 39:25 there is the phrase "Ha, ha!"

There's no mention of Eve eating an apple.

"Bible" is derived from the Greek word *biblion* meaning "book."

There are handwritten copies of the Bible so small that they could fit into a walnut shell.

THE ALBATROSS
10 writers living in the shadow of their "big" book

Bram Stoker: *Dracula*
Harriet Beecher Stowe: *Uncle Tom's Cabin*
J. P. Donleavy: *The Ginger Man*
Jonathan Swift: *Gulliver's Travels*
Erich Maria Remarque: *All Quiet on the Western Front*
Mario Puzo: *The Godfather*
J. D. Salinger: *The Catcher in the Rye*
Margaret Mitchell: *Gone with the Wind*
Mary Shelley: *Frankenstein*
Joseph Heller: *Catch 22*

BIOPICS

25 stars who played writers in films

Gregory Peck: Ambrose Bierce in *Old Gringo*
Chris O'Donnell: Ernest Hemingway in *In Love and War*
Daniel Day-Lewis: Christy Brown in *My Left Foot*
Gregory Peck: F. Scott Fitzgerald in *Beloved Infidel*
Jane Fonda: Lillian Hellman in *Julia*
Jason Robards: Dashiell Hammett in *Julia*
Herbert Marshall: W. Somerset Maugham in *The Razor's Edge*
Jack Nicholson: Eugene O'Neill in *Reds*
James Mason: Gustave Flaubert in *Madame Bovary*
Vanessa Redgrave: Agatha Christie in *Agatha*
Olivia de Havilland: Charlotte Brontë in *Devotion*
Judy Davis: George Sand in *Impromptu*
Malcolm McDowell: H. G. Wells in *Time after Time*
Gary Oldman: Joe Orton in *Prick up Your Ears*
Fred Ward: Henry Miller in *Henry and June*
Meryl Streep: Karen Blixen in *Out of Africa*
Leonardo DiCaprio: Arthur Rimbaud in *Total Eclipse*
Willem Dafoe: T. S. Eliot in *Tom and Viv*
Stephen Fry: Oscar Wilde in *Wilde*
Anthony Hopkins: C. S. Lewis in *Shadowlands*
Joseph Fiennes: William Shakespeare in *Shakespeare in Love*
Danny Kaye: Hans Christian Andersen in *Hans Christian Andersen*
Nick Nolte: Neal Cassady in *Heart Beat*
Johnny Depp: Hunter S. Thompson in *Fear and Loathing in Las Vegas*
David Thewlis: Paul Verlaine in *Total Eclipse*

A WOMB WITH A VIEW

10 surprising places of birth

J. R. R. Tolkien (South Africa)
Lawrence Durrell (India)
J. P. Donleavy (America)
Doris Lessing (Persia)
Joseph Conrad (Poland)
Tom Stoppard (Czechoslovakia)
Nevil Shute (Norway)
Hugh Walpole (New Zealand)
H. H. Munro, "Saki" (Burma)
Charles Bukowski (Germany)

BOOKS FOR CHANGE

10 books that have changed peoples lives more than any others (at least, according to *Time* magazine, September 1998)

The Autobiography of Malcolm X (1965)
Civilisation and its Discontents (Sigmund Freud, 1930)
The Common Sense Book of Baby and Child Care
    (Benjamin Spock, 1946)
Democracy and Education (John Dewey, 1916)
The Diary of a Young Girl (Anne Frank, 1947)
The General Theory of Employment, Interest and Money
    (John Maynard Keynes, 1936)
The Gulag Archipelago (Alexander Solzhenitsyn, 1974)
The Other America (Michael Harrington, 1962)

The Second Sex (Simone de Beauvoir, 1949)
Silent Spring (Rachel Carson, 1962)

AT TWO WITH NATURE

10 literary bisexuals

LORD BYRON

Initiated into heterosexual sex at the tender age of 11 by his family nurse, Byron ran the gamut of sexual activities from incest to attempted rape, and also enjoyed cavorting with young boys.

ANDRÉ GIDE

His first sexual experience was at 23 with a 14-year-old boy. He later had sex with a 16-year-old female prostitute but didn't enjoy that as much, his imagination transforming her into her little brother.

GIACOMO CASANOVA

Though his main reputation rests on his predilection for orgiastic heterosexual sex, he was expelled from a seminary in 1744 for homosexual acts.

W. SOMERSET MAUGHAM

Was married and had affairs with many women, but evidence suggests that his primary penchant was a homosexual—or even a pederast—one. He repressed his homosexual side as a young man for fear of being imprisoned like Oscar Wilde, but in later years he indulged it, expressing a preference for young school-boys—again, like Wilde.

PAUL VERLAINE

Was involved in an apparently stable marriage in 1870, but the following year he met Arthur Rimbaud and fell in love.

OSCAR WILDE

Wilde is primarily known as a homosexual, but he genuinely loved his wife Constance, who gave him two sons. The routine of marriage bored him, however, and the recurrence of his syphilis precluded him from having sex with Constance after a certain time. His homosexual side took over in his later years, perhaps as a result of anger over having contracted syphilis from a prostitute. (The poet Ernest Dowson brought him to a brothel in France near the end of his life, but Oscar likened the experience to "cold mutton." He asked Dowson, however, to relate the story in England, claiming that it would "entirely restore my character.")

D. H. LAWRENCE

Even though he was married and had many other sexual experiences with women, he once said that the closest he had come to perfect love was "with a young coal-miner when I was about 16."

YUKIO MISHIMA

Copulated freely with men, women, and boys.

CARSON MCCULLERS

Had several affairs with female writers, yet she was married twice (both times to the same man).

BRENDAN BEHAN

Irish-born sailor and would-be actor Peter Arthurs wrote a book detailing a sexual affair they had in America while Behan was married to Beatrice.

I CAN'T GO ON, I MUST GO ON, I'LL GO ON

5 cases of writer's block

WILLIAM WORDSWORTH

After the death of Robert Southey in 1843, he became poet laureate but he never wrote a single line of poetry in the seven years he held the post.

ERNEST HEMINGWAY

Suffered intermittent blockages throughout his life. They became more pronounced toward the end, when his drinking spiraled out of control and the neuroses and depressions that plagued him during his last decade took root.

G. K. CHESTERTON

Whenever he became blocked, he got up from his desk, took up his bow, and fired arrows from it through a window at a tree that was in his yard.

W. B. YEATS

His muse deserted him periodically during the 1890s, after Maud Gonne MacBride, the love of his life and sometime *femme inspiratrice*, rejected his romantic overtures.

GRAHAM GREENE

Had an unusual solution for it: he kept a dream diary. "In periods when I can't write," he once said, "I keep a notepad beside my bed. When I wake up in the night after having a dream, I note it down at once. I've discovered that dreams are like serials and the installments sometimes carry on for weeks and in the end form a whole."

LORDS OF THE RING
5 writers who were also proficient boxers

Arthur Conan Doyle
Samuel Johnson
Ezra Pound
Ernest Hemingway
George Bernard Shaw

POET'S CORNER
10 writers buried in Westminster Abbey

Charles Dickens
Thomas Hardy
Ben Jonson
Samuel Johnson
Rudyard Kipling
R. B. Sheridan
Geoffrey Chaucer
Edmund Spenser
Robert Browning
Alfred Lord Tennyson

FOREIGN FIELDS
15 authors buried abroad

John Keats (the Protestant Cemetery in Rome)
Edward Lear (San Remo Cemetery, Italy)
Tobias Smollett (the English Cemetery in Leghorn, Italy)
Robert Louis Stevenson (on the peak of Mount Vaea in Samoa)
Henry Fielding (the English Protestant Cemetery, Lisbon)
Oscar Wilde (Père Lachaise Cemetery, Paris)
Rupert Brooke (Skyros in the Aegean)
W. H. Auden (Kirchstatten, Austria)
Aubrey Beardsley (Menton Cathedral, France)
Samuel Beckett (Montparnasse Cemetery, Paris)
James Joyce (Fluntern, Switzerland)
Elizabeth Barrett Browning (the English Cemetery, Florence)
Ezra Pound (San Michele Cemetery, Venice)
George Gissing (Saint-Jean-de-Luz, France)
D. H. Lawrence (San Cristobal, New Mexico)

DOWN AND OUT IN PARIS
10 writers buried in Père Lachaise

Oscar Wilde
Alice B. Toklas
Gertrude Stein
Marcel Proust
Molière

Jean de La Fontaine
Alphonse Daudet
Colette
Guillaume Apollinaire
Honoré de Balzac

ASHES TO ASHES
10 books that were burned

Burning other people's

The New York Post Office authorities were so shocked by the first English-language edition of *Ulysses* that they burned all copies of it in 1922. James Joyce, who had already experienced outraged readers burning *Dubliners* some years before, commented, "This is the second time I have had the pleasure of being burned while on earth. I hope it means I shall pass through the fires of purgatory unscathed."

After his death, Gerard Manley Hopkins' final poems were burned, on the instructions of his religious order.

Copies of John Milton's books were burned publicly in 1660 because he was critical of Charles II.

Islamic fundamentalists across the world burned copies of Salman Rushdie's *The Satanic Verses* when a *fatwa* was imposed on him in 1988.

In May 1933, Hitler's backshooter Dr. Goebbels lit a huge bonfire in Berlin, where (primarily Jewish and communist) the works of authors like Einstein, Freud, Gorky, Lenin, Hemingway, Marx, Proust, and countless others went up in smoke. More than 2,000 books were burned in all.

Burning your own

When Thomas Carlyle sent his *History of the French Revolution* to John Stuart Mill to read, Mill's maid burned it for waste paper. There was no copy, but he rewrote it in six months. Mill offered Carlyle £200 compensation, as he was racked with guilt. Carlyle was loath to take it, but eventually accepted £100.

Sir Walter Raleigh burned a volume of his *History of the World* in a fit of depression one day. He was in jail and had just seen a murder take place outside his cell window. His version of the killing differed substantially from that of two other eyewitnesses, and he thought to himself: "What chance have I of giving a true picture of the world's history when three eyewitnesses to something that took place just five minutes ago can't agree!"

When Molière was in the process of translating Lucretius's *On the Nature of Things*, one of his servants casually picked up some of the pages and used them as curlpapers for Molière's wig. Molière was so enraged that he threw the rest of the manuscript into the fire.

After his death, Sir Richard Burton's wife Isabel burned his 1,282-page translation of *The Perfumed Garden* because she objected to its eroticism. Fired with anger, she went on to destroy twenty-six of his other books as well, including all his journals and diaries, making a pyre in the backyard of their villa in 1890.

Gore Vidal's house burned down when he was writing his third Edgar Box thriller. When he tried to start writing it again, he couldn't remember who the murderer was.

C

PURRFECT!
5 writers' relationships to cats

SAMUEL JOHNSON
His devotion to felines caused a certain tension in his relationship with his friend and biographer James Boswell, who was a confirmed cat hater.

EDWARD LEAR
Was so concerned with the sensitivities of his tomcat Foss that, when he changed house one time, he modeled his new abode exactly on the old one so that Foss wouldn't feel out of place.

EDGAR ALLAN POE
Was so devoted to Catarina, his favorite cat, that when he was away he would often write to her. She went off her food at such times, out of loneliness, but when he came back her excitement knew no bounds. (She also used to sit on his shoulder as he wrote.)

COLETTE
Was so besotted that she had up to a dozen of them living with her. She also took in strays and neighbors' cats when they were on vacation.

RAYMOND CHANDLER
Had a black Persian called Taki, whom he referred to as his secretary. The cat stayed loyally beside him when he was writing —usually sitting on his paper.

STRONGER THAN FICTION
10 fictional characters that live beyond the page

DON QUIXOTE
Cervantes' hero has become the model for an impractical idealist.

WALTER MITTY
James Thurber's daydreamer refers to anyone given to grand and elaborate fantasies.

MR. MICAWBER
From *David Copperfield*, Dickens' eternal optimist refers to anyone who idles and puts their hope and trust to fortune.

JEKYLL AND HYDE
A portmanteau term for anyone or anything with a schizoid or split personality.

LOTHARIO
Describes anyone who fancies themselves as a rake and a seducer extraordinaire. From Nicholas Rowe's *The Fair Penitent* (1703). See also: Don Juan, Romeo.

SCROOGE
Dickens' Christmas-hating old curmudgeon has come to represent grumps and misers everywhere.

THE SCARLET PIMPERNEL
Used to refer to anybody enigmatic, mysterious, and elusive. After Baroness Orczy's romantic royalist hero of revolutionary France.

SHYLOCK
Shakespeare's moneylending Jewish caricature from *The Merchant of Venice* who claims his pound of flesh. The name has come to refer to any heartless or demanding creditor.

UNCLE TOM
Shorthand for a black person who behaves subserviently towards whites. From Harriet Beecher Stowe's novel, *Uncle Tom's Cabin* (1852).

POOTER
After Charles Pooter, the Victorian clerk in George Grossmith's comic classic, *The Diary of a Nobody*. Describes a certain absurd and small-minded bourgeois self-importance.

SOMETHING FOR EVERYONE
10 authors who wrote for children as well as adults

RUDYARD KIPLING
Apart from his two jungle books, he wrote three other children's books: *Just So Stories*, *Rewards of the Fairies*, and *Puck of Pook's Hill*.

SALMAN RUSHDIE
Wrote his first children's book, *Haroun and the Sea of Stories*, in 1990, two years after the Ayatollah Khomeini had put a price on his head.

MARIA EDGEWORTH
Edgeworth's father had four wives and twenty-two children in all, so she was never short of immediate readers for her children's books. In 1976, she published a collection of stories called *The Parent's Assistant*, which was followed five years later by another collection, *Early Lessons and Moral Tales*.

OSCAR WILDE
As well as writing a string of plays with acerbic lines to die for, Ireland's favorite homosexual also wrote—no pun intended— fairy tales.

IAN FLEMING
He wrote *Chitty Chitty Bang Bang* as well as his more famous James Bond adventures.

T. S. ELIOT
Broke away from his familiarly morose introspection in 1939 to pen the serendipitous *Old Possum's Book of Practical Cats*.

EDWARD LEAR
Lear is probably better known for his children's books—*A Book of Nonsense, More Nonsense Rhymes*—than anything else, but he also wrote travel books for adults, like *Views in Rome* and *Illustrated Excursions in Italy*.

HILAIRE BELLOC
Known primarily for his adult writings, he also wrote children's verse such as *Cautionary Tales for Children* and *The Bad Child's Book of Beasts*.

P. G. WODEHOUSE
Long before he created Jeeves and Wooster, P. G. Wodehouse started out writing books about schoolboy heroes, Mike and Psmith.

BRAM STOKER
Published a collection of children's stories in 1882 called *Under the Sunset*, but even these were undercut by his penchant for the macabre. (He went on to create *Dracula*, of course, thirteen years later.)

WRITER'S BLOCK
5 writers who regularly suffered from constipation

Aldous Huxley
Marcel Proust
Sigmund Freud
Samuel Pepys
James Joyce

RIGHTS AND WRONGS
5 copyright curiosities

Thomas Babington Macaulay showed a lapse of savoir-faire in 1842 when he gave the copyright of *The Lays of Ancient Rome* free to his publisher, imagining that it would have very limited sales. The poem sold 100,000 copies over the next twenty-five years, which left him something to think about, although his publisher was gracious enough to return the copyright to him as well as cutting him in for some of the profits.

H. Rider Haggard was offered £100 to sell the copyright of *King Solomon's Mines* and he accepted, but just before signing on the dotted line he changed his mind. His instinct proved right, as sales of the book rocketed, topping 30,000 after a year. Haggard had been sorely tempted to accept the flat fee, in view of the fact that his writing career was going badly, but his snap decision to go for a 10 percent royalty contract instead made him rich.

Publisher Nicholas Parsons once bought the rights from United Artists to commission a series of novels based on the movie *The Magnificent Seven*. However, the United Artists contract was so dense (longer than the first novel, in fact) that he abandoned the idea.

John Milton's widow sold the copyright of *Paradise Lost* for £8 after he died.

In 1846, Edgar Allan Poe offered to sell the copyright of a collection of his stories for as little as $50. (His stars were on the wane at the time. Stranger still, the offer was rejected.)

CYNICAL SCRIBES
10 depressing views on the writing game

"You can't learn how to write. People who spend money on writing courses would do much better to send the money to me and I'll introduce them to an editor."

Fran Lebowitz

"I wonder if what we're publishing now is worth cutting down trees to make paper for the stuff?"

Richard Brautigan

"A book is a mirror. If an ass peers into it, you can't expect an apostle to look out."

G. C. Lichtenberg

"A writer appears before the public with his pants down. If it is a good book, nothing can hurt him. If it is a bad book, nothing can help him."

Edna St. Vincent Millay

"The instinct to write books is the same as the instinct that makes a baby squall for attention."

George Orwell

"Finishing a book is just like taking a child out into the garden and shooting it."

Truman Capote

"Writing is so difficult that I often feel that writers, having had their hell on earth, will escape all punishment hereafter."

Jessamyn West

"Literature is one vast hypocrisy, a giant deception. All writers have concealed more than they reveal."

Anaïs Nin

"What no wife of a writer can ever understand is that he's working when he's staring out the window."

Burton Roscoe

"Sometimes I think authors should write one book and then be put in the gas chamber."

John P. Marquand

D

SHORT STORIES

10 writers who died before they reached 40

ROBERT BURNS
Died of rheumatic heart disease at 36.

CHARLOTTE BRONTË
At 39, from tuberculosis. (Her sister Emily died at 30 from the same disease, and Anne died from it also, at 29.)

KATHERINE MANSFIELD
At 34, of a pulmonary hemorrhage.

JOHN MILLINGTON SYNGE
At 38, of a lymphatic tumor.

ARTHUR RIMBAUD
At 37, of syphilis.

AUBREY BEARDSLEY
At 25, from tuberculosis.

STEPHEN CRANE
At 28, of tuberculosis.

DYLAN THOMAS
Drank himself to death at 39.

JOHN KEATS
At 25, from tuberculosis.

RAYMOND RADIGUET
Died at 20, from typhoid fever.

10 writers who died in their 40s

F. SCOTT FITZGERALD
At 44, of a heart attack.

GEORGE ORWELL
At 46, from tuberculosis.

GUY DE MAUPASSANT
From syphilis, at 43.

CHARLES BAUDELAIRE
At 46, from the combined effects of drug addiction and syphilis.

JANE AUSTEN
At 43, from consumption.

ROBERT LOUIS STEVENSON
At 44, from a cerebral hemorrhage.

BRENDAN BEHAN
From a combination of alcohol and diabetes, at 42.

OSCAR WILDE
Contracted meningitis after an ear infection, at the age of 46.

D. H. LAWRENCE
At 44, from tuberculosis.

EDGAR ALLAN POE
At 40, from a combination of alcohol and epilepsy.

AS I LAY DYING

10 writers who departed in mysterious ways

SHERWOOD ANDERSON
Choked to death on a toothpick.

ARNOLD BENNETT
Drank water from a carafe in a Paris restaurant in an attempt to show that the city's water was safe to drink, but he caught typhoid from it and died two months later.

MOLIÈRE
Was playing the lead role of the hypochondriac in his play *The Imaginary Invalid* when he died. Which just goes to show…

AESCHYLUS
Is alleged to have died when an eagle dropped a tortoise on his head.

EMILE ZOLA
Asphyxiated by carbon monoxide fumes from a fire in his bedroom (it had a defective chimney) in 1902, aged 62.

PIETRO ARETINO
This Italian satirist poet literally laughed himself to death at the theater one night in 1556: he fell off his seat and fatally banged his head on the floor.

THOMAS MERTON
This prolific Cistercian monk was electrocuted by a faulty fan while attending a conference on Buddhism in Bangkok.

FRANCIS BACON
Killed a chicken one day and stuffed its carcass with snow in an effort to discover if chilled meat could be preserved in this fashion. An innovative idea for the time … but the chicken fared better than him, as he caught a fatal chill while he was stuffing it.

RAINER MARIA RILKE
Died at the age of 51 of blood poisoning, after he had been cut by the thorn of a rose he had picked for a woman he knew.

TENNESSEE WILLIAMS
Choked to death on the plastic top of a nasal spray in a New York hotel room in 1983.

AFTER THE WAKE?
10 posthumous oddities

D. H. LAWRENCE
After he died, his wife Frieda had his ashes tipped into a concrete mixer and incorporated them into the altar of their private chapel.

AUGUST STRINDBERG
Was born the year Edgar Allan Poe died, and often claimed that Poe's spirit had entered his body and inspired his writing.

PERCY BYSSHE SHELLEY
After he died, his wife had his heart preserved. She wrapped it in silk and carried it with her wherever she went.

GABRIELE D'ANNUNZIO
When his inamorata Eleanor Duse died, he said that he would communicate with her spirit by biting into a pomegranate while standing in front of a statue of Buddha.

HILAIRE BELLOC
Was so distraught after the death of his wife that he wrote all of his subsequent works on mourning paper.

JOHN MILTON
His grave was raided in 1790 and an opportunist started to charge voyeuristic onlookers sixpence a go to see his teeth and part of his leg.

ALFRED LORD TENNYSON
When he was a child, he had a death wish and spent a lot of time in a graveyard outside the church where his father was a rector, lying prostrate among the headstones.

VIRGIL
Once held a lavish funeral for his favorite pet fly.

GEORGE BERNARD SHAW
Left money in his will to help implement a new alphabet with phonetic spelling—a lifetime obsession.

EDITH SOMERVILLE
After her writing partner Martin Ross died in 1915, Somerville continued to publish her subsequent books under both names, feeling that the spirit of her deceased collaborator was still working through her.

HOPELESSLY DEVOTED TO YOU
15 famous literary dedications

CHARLES LAMB
Dedicated his *Essays of Elia* to Samuel Taylor Coleridge.

PERCY BYSSHE SHELLEY
Dedicated *Adonis* to John Keats.

HERMAN MELVILLE
Dedicated *Moby Dick* to Nathaniel Hawthorne.

IVAN TURGENEV
Dedicated *A Song of Triumphant Love* to Flaubert.

OLIVER GOLDSMITH
Dedicated *She Stoops to Conquer* to Samuel Johnson.

ANAÏS NIN
Dedicated *Ladders to Fire* to Gore Vidal in appreciation of the fact that he got her published by E. P. Dutton when she was struggling for recognition. (The dedication was removed from later editions of the book.)

CHARLES BAUDELAIRE
Dedicated *Les Fleurs du Mal* to his friend Theophile Gautier.

GEOFFREY CHAUCER
Dedicated *Troilus and Cressida* to the poet John Gower.

LEO TOLSTOY
Dedicated *Woodfelling* to Turgenev.

JOSEPH CONRAD
Dedicated *The Secret Agent* to H. G. Wells.

WILLIAM MAKEPEACE THACKERAY
Dedicated *Barry Lyndon* to Henry Fielding.

AGATHA CHRISTIE
Dedicated *Halloween Party* to P. G. Wodehouse.

WILLIAM FAULKNER
Dedicated *Sanctuary* to Sherwood Anderson for services rendered. (Anderson had recommended Faulkner's first novel, *Soldier's Pay*, to a publisher on condition that he didn't have to read it himself: surely a backhanded compliment.)

TRUMAN CAPOTE
Dedicated *Music for Chameleons* to Tennessee Williams.

CHARLOTTE BRONTË
Dedicated *Jane Eyre* to William Makepeace Thackeray.

WITH GRATITUDE ...
5 curious dedications

WILLIAM FAULKNER
The notorious southern tippler inscribed a copy of *As I Lay Dying*, "With gratitude to Dr. Cointreau, the translator."

NIKOLAUS PEVSNER
Dedicated his book *Bedfordshire, Huntingdon and Peterborough* to the inventor of the popsicle.

LARRY MCMURTRY
The Desert Rose carries this rather odd attribution: "To Lesley, for the use of her goat."

FELIX RAOUL LEBLANC
Wrote a book on the prevention of venereal disease and "affectionately" dedicated it to his wife.

E. E. CUMMINGS
Dedicated his aptly titled book *No Thanks* to the fourteen publishers who had rejected it ... and also to his mother, who (much more importantly) paid for its printing.

WATCHING THE DETECTIVES
15 classic detectives and their creators

SIMON TEMPLAR (THE SAINT)
(Leslie Charteris)

SHERLOCK HOLMES
(Sir Arthur Conan Doyle)

PHILIP MARLOWE
(Raymond Chandler)

PERRY MASON
(Earle Stanley Gardner)

SAM SPADE
(Dashiell Hammett)

INSPECTOR MAIGRET
(Georges Simenon)

HERCULE POIROT
(Agatha Christie)

CHARLIE CHAN
(Earl Biggers)

JANE MARPLE
(Agatha Christie)

BULLDOG DRUMMOND
(Herman Cyril McNeil)

LEW ARCHER
(John Ross MacDonald)

LORD PETER WIMSEY
(Dorothy L. Sayers)

ALBERT CAMPION
(Margery Allingham)

MIKE HAMMER
(Mickey Spillane)

FATHER BROWN
(G. K. Chesterton)

QUEER REMARKS

10 unintentional *double-entendres* from the classics

"Mrs. Glegg had doubtless the glossiest and crispest brown curls in her drawers, as well as curls in various degrees of fuzzy laxness." (George Eliot, *The Mill on the Floss*)

"'My master,' he says, 'has forewarned me. Daily he announces more distinctly, 'Surely I come quickly' and hourly I more eagerly respond, 'Amen! Even so, come, Lord Jesus!'"
(Charlotte Brontë, *Jane Eyre*)

"She touched his organ, and from that bright epoch even it, the old companion of his happiest hours, incapable as he had thought of elevation, began a new and defined existence."
(Charles Dickens, *Martin Chuzzlewit*)

"I'll come no more behind your scenes, David, for the silk stockings and white bosoms of your actresses excite my amorous propensities." (Samuel Johnson in conversation with David Garrick in *Boswell's Life of Dr. Johnson*)

"Prince of the school, he had gained an easy dominion over the old Greek master by the fascination of his parts." (Walter Pater, *Marius the Epicurean*)

"Mrs. Goddard was the mistress of a school ... where young ladies for enormous pay might be screwed out of health and into vanity." (Jane Austen, *Emma*)

"You think me a queer fellow already. It's not easy to tell you how I feel, not easy for so queer a fellow as I to tell you in how many ways he's queer." (Henry James, *A Passionate Pilgrim*)

"'Well,' said the duchess, 'apart from your balls, can't I be of any use to you?'" (Marcel Proust, *Cities of the Plain*)

"'Oh I can't explain,' cried Roderick impatiently, returning to his work. 'I've only one way of expressing my deepest feelings— it's this.' And he swung his tool." (Henry James, *Roderick Hudson*)

"Mrs. Ray declared that she had not found it all hard, and then, with a laudable curiosity, seeing how little she had known about balls, desired to have an immediate account of Rachel's doings." (Anthony Trollope, *Rachel Ray*)

5 unintentional *double-entendres* in book titles

Flashes from the Welsh Pulpit
This 1889 offering from Hodder and Stoughton wasn't the first in a series of clerical scandals, but was, in fact, a much more boring anthology of didactic titbits.

British Tits
Not the exposé of topless models you might have wished for; only a suggestive ornithological survey from Christopher Perrins in 1979.

Under Two Queens
You'd be advised not to take the title of this 1884 book from John Huntley Skrine literally—it's just another royal-matching exercise … unfortunately.

The Gay Boys of Old Vale
John Denison Vose wrote this university memoir in 1869, more than a century before the eponymous adjective had attained its homosexual overtones.

Making it in Leather
M. Vincent Hayes wrote this in 1972—not for the S/M brigade, but for the home improvement market.

WATERY GRAVES
5 writers who drowned

JOHN BERRYMAN
Jumped to his death from a bridge in Minneapolis in 1972.

PERCY BYSSHE SHELLEY
Drowned when a storm hit his sail boat in 1822. He had a copy of Keats' poetry in his pocket when his body was found. (His wife Mary also drowned, but in her case it was suicide.)

VIRGINIA WOOLF
Drowned herself in the River Ouse in 1941 after a lifetime of mental turmoil. She filled her pockets with pebbles in order to weigh herself down.

HART CRANE
Threw himself off a ship in 1932 (on the way back from Mexico to New York) as the result of confused sexuality, depression over his writing, and increasingly heavy drinking. (His father, ironically, was the inventor of "Lifesavers" candy.) Tennessee Williams requested that, after his own death, he should be cremated and his ashes scattered over the Caribbean Sea just at the point where Crane leaped off the ship.

LI PO
This Chinese poet met the Grim Reaper when, on a boat one night, he reached over the edge to kiss the reflection of the moon on the water, fell in, and drowned.

3

THE BRAT PACK

10 authors who began their writing careers early

VICTOR HUGO
Wrote his first play when he was only 14.

ALFRED JARRY
Had completed the first draft of *Ubu Roi* by the time he was 15.

JACK KEROUAC
Wrote his first novel at the age of 11.

ALFRED LORD TENNYSON
Started composing poetry at the age of 5 and had written a 6,000-word poem by the time he was 10.

JOHANN GOETHE
Wrote a story in seven different languages when he was 10.

SIDNEY SHELDON
Sold his first poem when he was 10. Eight years later, he was working in Hollywood as a screenwriter.

JORGE LUIS BORGES
By the age of 9 he had translated Oscar Wilde's *The Happy Prince* into Spanish.

JACK LONDON
Won a competition with his first story in the San Francisco *Morning Call* at the age of 17, pocketing $25.

LANGSTON HUGHES
Wrote his first poem at the age of 13 and was instantly elected class poet.

ANAÏS NIN
Began her celebrated diary at the age of 11 in 1914.

BIZARRE BEHAVIOR
15 assorted literary eccentrics

PERCY BYSSHE SHELLEY
Hated cats so much that he once tied a tomcat to a kite in a thunderstorm in the hopes of seeing it electrocuted.

RUDYARD KIPLING
Once painted his golf balls red so that he could play in the snow.

H. G. WELLS
Always carried two pens with him: a big one for long words, he claimed, and a smaller one for the little ones.

THOMAS DE QUINCEY
Tended to become so immersed in what he was writing that he often set his hair and/or clothes on fire from the candle he placed by his writing desk.

ALFRED LORD TENNYSON
One of his party pieces was imitating a person sitting on a toilet.

DOROTHY PARKER
Once bought herself a new typewriter for no better reason than the fact that the ribbon on her old one ran out and she didn't know how to fit another one to the machine.

GIACOMO CASANOVA
Used to grow the nail on his pinkie extralong so that he could pick out earwax with it.

WILLIAM WORDSWORTH
Once wallpapered an entire room with newspapers.

GEORGE BERNARD SHAW

Once began a letter to Ellen Terry like this: "Ellen, Ellen, Ellen, Ellen, Ellen, Ellen, Ellen, Ellen, Ellen, Eleanor, Eleanest …".

J. M. BARRIE

Always ordered Brussels sprouts for lunch, but he never ate them. When asked the reason for this, he replied, "I love saying the words."

SAMUEL BECKETT

Said to an actor in one of his plays (apropos a pregnant silence): "You're playing two dots at the moment; the script says three."

T. S. ELIOT

Was playing solitaire one day when spotted by W. H. Auden. Auden asked him why he liked the game. "Because it's the closest experience to being dead," Eliot replied.

CHARLES DICKENS

Used to get so excited performing his own work onstage that he sometimes fainted.

SAMUEL JOHNSON

Once shaved all the hairs off his arms and chest to see how long it would take for them to grow back again.

DIOGENES

Roamed the streets in broad daylight with a lantern looking for that rare thing: an honest man.

DO UNTO OTHERS ...

15 writers who were also editors

EDGAR ALLAN POE
In his capacity as editor of the *Southern Literary Messenger*, he built up its circulation from 500 to 3,500 copies. When editing *Graham's* magazine, he increased the readership from 5,000 to 35,000.

GEORGE ORWELL
Literary editor of *Tribune* in 1943.

HILAIRE BELLOC
Literary editor of the *Morning Post* from 1905 to 1910.

FINLEY PETER DUNNE
Editor of *Collier's* from 1918 to 1919.

CHARLES DICKENS
Founder and editor of the *Daily News*.

FYODOR DOSTOEVSKI
Edited the *Citizen* from 1873 to 1874.

W. SOMERSET MAUGHAM
Founder and editor of the *Legal Observer*.

ROBERT BENCHLEY
Former managing editor of *Vanity Fair*.

MARTIN AMIS
Editor of the *New Statesman* from 1977 to 1978.

MURIEL SPARK
Editor of *Poetry Review* from 1947 to 1949.

ROBERT PENN WARREN
Editor of the *Southern Review*.

MARK TWAIN

After working on several frontier newspapers in Nevada and California (where he first used his pseudonym), he became editor and part-owner of the *Buffalo Express* back east in the 1870s.

G. K. CHESTERTON

Editor of *New Witness* from 1916 to 1923 and *G.K.'s Weekly* from 1925 to 1936.

BEN HECHT

Edited the *Chicago Literary Times* from 1923 to 1924.

H. L. MENCKEN

Editor of the *Baltimore Herald* in 1906.

PAPER CUTS

15 writers on editors and editing

"I have made this letter longer than usual only because I have not had the time to make it shorter."

Blaise Pascal

"The writer must be able to see where he was lying to himself, where his mouth was full of sawdust instead of grapes, where his gunpowder was only snuff."

Peter Straub

"Every author's fairy godmother should provide him not only with a pen but also with a blue pencil."

F. L. Lucas

"Anyone who can improve a sentence of mine by the omission or placing of a comma is my dearest friend."

George Moore

"An editor should have a pimp for a brother so he'd have someone to look up to."

Gene Fowler

"An editor's job is to send checks. They should also praise you. Every time you hand something in they should say it's the best thing you've ever written."

Fran Lebowitz

"You never have to change anything you got up in the middle of the night to write."

Saul Bellow

"Crappy work I do twice; good work, three times."

Paul Fussell

"No passion in the world, in love or hate, is equal to the passion to alter someone else's copy."

H. G. Wells

"My definition of a good editor is a man who sends me large checks, praises my work, my physical beauty, and sexual prowess, and who has a stranglehold on the publisher and the bank."

John Cheever

"A good many young writers make the mistake of enclosing a stamped self-addressed envelope with their manuscript which is big enough for it to come back in. This is far too much of a temptation for any editor."

Ring Lardner

"The last paragraph in which you tell what the story is about is almost always best left out."

Irwin Shaw

"On the day the young writer corrects his first proof sheet he is as proud as a schoolboy who has just gotten his first dose of the pox."

Charles Baudelaire

"I was working on the proof of one of my poems all morning and I took out a comma. In the afternoon I put it back in again."

Oscar Wilde

"The chief qualification of ninety percent of all editors is failure. They have failed as writers, and right there is the cursed paradox of it. Every portal to literature is guarded by those watchdogs."

Jack London

VANITY FAIR
10 examples of the writer's ego

"The quality which makes a man want to write and be read is essentially a desire for self-exposure—like one of those guys who has a compulsion to take his thing out and show it on the street."

James Jones

"I wrote my first novel because I wanted to read it."

Toni Morrison

"Every author, however modest, keeps a most outrageous vanity chained like a madman in the padded cell of his breast."

Logan Pearsall Smith

"Whatever has been well said by anyone is mine."

Seneca

"I often quote myself. It adds spice to my conversation."

George Bernard Shaw

"The books I haven't written are better than the books other people have."

Cyril Connolly

"For several days after my first book was published I carried it about in my pocket, taking surreptitious peeps at it to make sure the ink had not faded."

J. M. Barrie

"Most people enjoy the sight of their own handwriting as they enjoy the smell of their own farts."

W. H. Auden

"I have never met an author who admitted that people did not buy his book because it was dull."

W. Somerset Maugham

"It does no harm to repeat to yourself as often as you can, 'Without me, the literary industry would not exist.'"

Doris Lessing

GRAVE MATTERS

5 epitaphs suggested by authors for themselves

Excuse my dust. (Dorothy Parker)
The defense rests. (John Mortimer)
Don't try it. (Charles Bukowski)
His first holiday. (Dion Boucicault)
This is over my head. (Robert Graves)

THE EXECUTIONER'S SONG
10 writers put to death by the State

CICERO
Was beheaded when he challenged the supremacy of Mark
Antony after the assassination of Julius Caesar in 44 B.C. Antony
also had Cicero's hands cut off and displayed on a rostrum, as a
warning to others who might write anything against him.

PIERRE PETIT
This salacious French author had the misfortune to leave the
window of his study open one day in the seventeenth century
and the wind blew away his poems. A priest was passing by his
door at the time and, after reading them and being suitably shocked,
submitted them to the authorities. The poems were then burned
… and so was poor Pierre.

PAORAIC PEARSE
This Irish teacher-poet spearheaded the 1916 insurrection against
the British during Easter week in Dublin, taking over the
General Post Office, alongside fellow revolutionaries. He was
executed afterward by firing squad, thus making him one of
Ireland's preeminent martyrs.

FEDERICO GARCÍA LORCA
Spain's most important poet of the twentieth century was shot by
Franco's troops after the outbreak of the Spanish Civil War in
1936. He was tortured first, then buried in an unmarked grave.

SIR WALTER RALEIGH
This naval commander (and author of *History of the World*) was
sentenced to death after the accession of James I in 1603, but not
executed until fifteen years later, on Tower Hill, where his head
was cut off and sent to his widow.

GIROLAMO SAVONAROLA
A Florentine preacher who fought against both the Medici rule and corrupt clergymen, Savonarola was condemned to be burned at the stake in 1498 for his fiery writings and speechifying.

SOCRATES
Poisoned by hemlock in 399 B.C. because of his unorthodox writings.

ROBERT ERSKINE CHILDERS
Author of *The Riddle of the Sands,* he was executed for treason by the Irish State in 1922 after becoming a Sinn Fein supporter.

MICHAEL SERVETUS
Servitus denied some central tenets of Christianity in his book *Christianismi Restitutio* in 1553. He was convicted by a court and burned at the stake, the book pinned to his arm as he died.

GIORDANO BRUNO
Arrested by the Inquisition and burned at the stake in Rome in 1600 for his unorthodox writings on science and religion.

THE OLD COUNTRY
5 Russian literary exiles

ALEXANDER SOLZHENITSYN
Exiled in 1974 for his exposé of Russian prison camps in *The Gulag Archipelago*. He was lucky not to be assassinated. Instead, he was stripped of his citizenship and flown to West Germany, where he was received by Heinrich Böll. From here he went to Zurich and then to the U.S.A. In 1989 he was readmitted to the Soviet Writers' Union and his citizenship was restored. After nearly two decades of exile, he returned to Russia with his family.

FYODOR DOSTOEVSKI
Charged with being part of a socialist conspiracy in 1849 and was sentenced to death. A reprieve, however, was granted even as he stood before the firing squad and he was exiled to Siberia instead.

IVAN TURGENEV
Exiled in 1852 for writing an apocryphal obituary of Gogol.

MIKHAIL LERMONTOV
Lermontov was a dashing young officer in a fashionable regiment in St. Petersburg, but he wrote a poem in 1837 denouncing Russian society for the death of Alexander Pushkin, who had been killed earlier that year in a duel. (Lermontov felt that his death had been deliberately engineered.) The poem was regarded as inflammatory by the authorities and they appointed Lermontov to a regiment in the Caucasus as a means of punishment. The following year, he fought in a duel himself and was exiled again.

VLADIMIR NABOKOV
This precocious child of St. Petersburg aristocrats was born in 1899. He and his family fled the country following the Bolshevik uprising in 1919.

A LONG WAY FROM HOME
5 other literary exiles

GIACOMO CASANOVA
Exiled from Italy in 1774 for writing a satire on the Neapolitan ruling class.

THOMAS PAINE
Exiled from England after the publication of *The Rights of Man*,
a book that supported the ideals of the French Revolution and
called for the overthrow of the British monarchy. He fled to
France in 1792 and joined the French National Convention.

DANTE ALIGHIERI
Involved in political infighting, he was banished from his native
Florence in 1309 and sentenced to death by burning in absentia
if he ever returned.

VICTOR HUGO
Exiled by Napoleon III in 1851, he lived in Guernsey for
nineteen years, where he wrote *Les Misérables*.

CELINE
Was arrested, tried, and extradited by the French Government in
1945, on charges of antisemitism. He was exonerated and
returned from exile six years later.

AWAY WITH WORDS
15 expatriate authors

D. H. LAWRENCE
Lawrence ran off to Germany with Frieda Weekley, the wife of
his former Modern Languages tutor in 1912 and married her on
his return to England, two years later, just as World War I broke
out. Anti-German feeling intensified his restlessness and in 1919
he went to Italy, feeling under constant surveillance. He also
traveled to Australia, Mexico, Sicily, and Ceylon.

MALCOLM LOWRY

Was born in Cheshire, England, but his nomadic life led him to France, Spain, America, and Mexico. He also spent some time in Canada, but was evicted from his house there in 1954 to make way for a public park.

ERNEST HEMINGWAY

Gravitated between Paris, Spain, Cuba, America, and Africa in a life characterized by wanderlust.

JOSEPH CONRAD

Born in the Russian-annexed Polish Ukraine, but his seafaring nature brought him first to Marseilles and then to the West Indies, the Far East, Australia, and, finally, England.

W. SOMERSET MAUGHAM

Grew up with French as his first language because his father worked in the British Embassy in Paris and traveled constantly to such countries as Italy, Mexico, Africa, China, India, and the South Sea Islands.

LORD BYRON

Left England in 1809 at the age of 21 and wandered the Mediterranean for two years. He returned, but left again in 1816 to live in Italy. He also traveled to Albania, Asia Minor, and Turkey. He died in Greece.

WILLIAM S. BURROUGHS

Was born in St. Louis but spent many years expatriated in Paris, London, Tangiers, and Mexico.

TRUMAN CAPOTE

A native of New Orleans, at one time or another he lived in Greece, Italy, Africa, and the West Indies, as well as traveling through Russia and the Far East.

GERTRUDE STEIN
Born in Pennsylvania in 1874, but traveled to London in 1902 and to Paris the following year. She stayed there for the rest of her life.

EZRA POUND
Was born in Idaho, but at the age of 23 went to Gibraltar on a cattle boat. Afterward he walked to Italy and, from there, went to London, Ireland, and France respectively.

J. P. DONLEAVY
Was born in Brooklyn, but has spent most of his life in Ireland.

HENRY JAMES
Born in New York, but he spent his formative years in cities like Geneva, London, Paris, and so on, soaking up the bohemian ambience. He returned to Boston in the early 1870s but felt strangely disorientated there, so he made a decision to settle in Europe for good. This he did, with the exception of two extended visits to the U.S.A. His last years were spent in Rye on the south coast of England.

ISAAC BASHEVIS SINGER
Born in Poland but emigrated to the U.S.A. in 1935, taking out American citizenship eight years later.

VLADIMIR NABOKOV
After fleeing Russia, the multilingual Nabokov lived and wrote in Berlin, then Paris, then the United States, and finally returned to Europe.

T. S. ELIOT
Born in Missouri but spent three years at the Sorbonne studying for a Ph.D. and, from there, went to England, where he became a naturalized citizen.

OUT OF IRELAND HAVE WE COME
10 Irish expatriate authors

JAMES JOYCE
Was often asked why he left Ireland, but he always gave the same answer: "Did I ever leave it?" (because he never wrote about anywhere else). He had a love-hate relationship with the country, leaving it because he felt it would paralyze his talent with its begrudgery and provincialism. He referred to it as "the old sow that eats her farrow," and also said, "It is dangerous to leave one's country but still more dangerous to go back to it, for then your fellow-countrymen will drive a knife into your heart."

GEORGE BERNARD SHAW
After being asked why he left Ireland, he replied: "England had conquered it, so I decided there was nothing for it but to come over and conquer England."

SEAN O'CASEY
Claimed Ireland was a terrible country to live in, but a great one to get a letter from. Moved to Devon in 1938 at the age of 58 and stayed there until he died.

BRENDAN BEHAN
Went to England on a bombing campaign for the IRA in his tender years but then achieved huge literary success there. "It's a great bloody country," he once said. "First they locked me up, then they made me rich."

SAMUEL BECKETT
Was in Dublin when World War II broke out, but left it for Paris, saying, "I would prefer France at war than Ireland at peace."

BRIAN MOORE
Emigrated to Canada in 1948 to become a Canadian citizen and lived there until his death, only rarely paying visits home to Ireland.

DION BOUCICAULT
Moved to New York in 1853 and stayed there until his death in 1890.

WILLIAM TREVOR
A native of Cork who has lived in England since 1954.

JAMES STEPHENS
Moved to London in 1937 and two years later went to New York, where he lived for the rest of his life, apart from occasional journeys home to Ireland.

EDNA O'BRIEN
Has lived in England for most of her life, but says she can't escape Ireland, even in her dreams: "And that's the way I like it."

EYELESS IN GAZA
15 writers who had problems with their eyes

JEAN-PAUL SARTRE
Became virtually blind toward the end of his life, which meant that he could "write" only by dictation.

WILLIAM WORDSWORTH
His eyesight was so poor by the time he reached middle age that he couldn't read for more than fifteen minutes at a time.

SAMUEL JOHNSON
Suffered from scrofula (tuberculosis of the lymphatic glands), which affected the sight in one of his eyes.

SAMUEL PEPYS
In 1669, his doctors informed him that his eyesight was so bad there was a danger he would go blind if he didn't give up writing the diary he had been working on for the past nine years. (Considering that it had reached 1.25 million words by then, perhaps this was nature's way of telling him to wrap it up.)

CARSON McCULLERS
A series of crippling strokes in her 20s caused her to lose the sight of her right eye. She was also partially paralyzed, which meant that her literary output was reduced to a page a day.

DANTE GABRIEL ROSSETTI
Chose an unusual way of dealing with his poor eyesight: he wore two pairs of specs.

ERNEST HEMINGWAY
Poor eyesight ran in the family, and in his case this explains many of the accidents he suffered throughout his life. (He was too vain to wear glasses.)

GABRIELE D'ANNUNZIO
Was blinded in the left eye by an enemy bullet when on a flying mission during World War I.

MARQUIS DE SADE
Lost the sight in one of his eyes when he was in jail.

FYODOR DOSTOEVSKI
Prone to attacks of epilepsy from his 20s: during one fit he injured his right eye, which caused it to be permanently distended.

SEAN O'CASEY
Suffered all his life from painful trachoma.

JAMES JOYCE
An attack of glaucoma in 1917 led to the first in an agonizing series of eye operations, which explains the patch he sometimes wore. He was also prone to iritis, which eventually got so bad that he had to learn to touch-type toward the end of his life; otherwise, he wouldn't have been able to write at all.

JOHN MILTON
Went blind at the age of 46, which meant that his greatest poem, *Paradise Lost*, could only be written with the help of his three daughters, who doubled as secretaries.

JORGE LUIS BORGES
Borges' father's literary career was cut short by blindness, and the hereditary condition eventually struck Jorge, too.

ALDOUS HUXLEY
Developed eye problems while at Eton, which left him virtually blind and prevented him from pursuing a career in science.

F

WHEN WORLDS COLLIDE
10 quotes on fact and fiction

"Truth may be stranger than fiction, but fiction is truer."

Frederic Raphael

"Nothing I wrote in the thirties saved one Jew from Auschwitz."

W. H. Auden

"Life resembles a novel more often than a novel resembles life."

George Sand

"There never was a good biography of a good novelist. There couldn't be. He is too many people if he's any good."

F. Scott Fitzgerald

"The trouble with fiction is that it makes too much sense, whereas reality never makes sense."

Aldous Huxley

"Books succeed, and lives fail."

Elizabeth Barrett Browning

"People say that life is the thing, but I prefer reading."

Logan Pearsall Smith

"Good writing excites me, and makes life worth living."

Harold Pinter

"Sometimes I don't know whether Zelda and I are real or whether we're characters in one of my novels."

F. Scott Fitzgerald

"There is no longer any such thing as fiction or nonfiction. There is only narrative."

E. L. Doctorow

OCCUPATIONAL HAZARDS
80 authors' fathers' jobs

Molière (Upholsterer)
Balzac (Hospital administrator)
J. M. Barrie (Hand-loom weaver)
Baudelaire (House painter)
Brendan Behan (Guard)
James Joyce (Official in tax office)
E. M. Forster (Architect)
Flaubert (Surgeon)
F. Scott Fitzgerald (Furniture salesman)
Patrick Kavanagh (Cobbler)
Brian Friel (Principal)
Samuel Beckett (Building contractor)
George Eliot (Bailiff)
Arthur Conan Doyle (Clerk)
Fyodor Dostoevski (Physician)
John Donne (Ironmonger)
Charles Dickens (Clerk)
Marquis de Sade (Soldier)
Thomas de Quincey (Linen merchant)
Daniel Defoe (Butcher)
R. B. Sheridan (Actor)
Wilkie Collins (Landscape painter)
Samuel Taylor Coleridge (Principal)
G. K. Chesterton (Auctioneer)
Anton Chekhov (Grocer)
Geoffrey Chaucer (Wine trader)
Miguel Cervantes (Apothecary surgeon)
Thomas Carlyle (Stonemason)

Robert Burns (Cottager)
Matthew Arnold (Principal)
Arnold Bennett (Pawnbroker)
Oscar Wilde (Eye specialist)
Bram Stoker (Clerk)
Seán O'Faoláin (Constable in the Royal Irish Constabulary)
Hugh Leonard (Gardener)
Robert Louis Stevenson (Lighthouse engineer)
Tobias Smollett (Landowner)
W. B. Yeats (Painter)
Shakespeare (Glover)
John Ruskin (Merchant)
Jean-Jacques Rousseau (Watchmaker)
Arthur Rimbaud (Army captain)
Mark Twain (Storekeeper)
Alexander Pushkin (Army major)
Marcel Proust (Physician)
Edgar Allan Poe (Actor)
Guy de Maupassant (Stockbroker)
Christopher Marlowe (Shoemaker)
Thomas Hardy (Stonemason)
Ernest Hemingway (Doctor)
Henrik Ibsen (Merchant)
Samuel Pepys (Tailor)
August Strindberg (Shipping agent)
Charles Lamb (Clerk)
Alexander Pope (Draper)
D. H. Lawrence (Coal miner)
Edward Lear (Stockbroker)
Thomas Moore (Grocer)
George Bernard Shaw (Civil servant)
Fyodor Dostoevski (Physician)

Sigmund Freud (Wool merchant)
Rudyard Kipling (Architect)
Thomas Wolfe (Stonecutter)
Emile Zola (Engineer)
John Dryden (Landowner)
Harold Pinter (Tailor)
Larry McMurtry (Cattleman)
Alan Sillitoe (Laborer)
Sinclair Lewis (Doctor)
Eugene O'Neill (Actor)
Noel Coward (Piano salesman)
Rainer Maria Rilke (Railway conductor)
H. G. Wells (Storekeeper)
Seamus Heaney (Farmer)
Samuel Johnson (Bookseller)
Hermann Hesse (Missionary)
Knut Hamsun (Shoemaker)
Jerome K. Jerome (Hardware dealer)
Tobias Wolff (Confidence man)
J. D. Salinger (Cheese importer)

HOLY FATHERS
10 writers whose fathers were clergymen

e.e. cummings
Ben Jonson
Andrew Marvell
Charlotte Brontë
William Cowper

Oliver Goldsmith
Jane Austen
George Farquhar
Samuel Taylor Coleridge
Alfred Lord Tennyson

PULP FRICTION
10 sets of literary feuders

DOROTHY PARKER AND CLARE BOOTHE LUCE
Parker never resisted an opportunity to attack her *bête noire*. One day she was going through a door with her. Luce gestured Parker to go first with the words "Age before beauty," to which Parker replied, "And pearls before swine," as she marched through. When someone pointed out to her that Luce was kind to her inferiors, Parker blurted out, "Where does she find them?"

JEAN-PAUL SARTRE AND ALBERT CAMUS
Theirs was always an uneasy relationship. Sartre admired Camus as a writer, but found his philosophizing flaky. He also had problems with what he deemed to be his preachiness and air of "somber self-importance." Camus, for his part, thought Sartre was bourgeois.

W. B. YEATS AND SEAN O'CASEY
After Yeats rejected O'Casey's play *The Silver Tassie* in 1928 – posterity has been kinder to it than the Abbey Theatre of that time – O'Casey left Ireland in a fit of pique, going into permanent exile in Devon. He found it difficult to forgive the man who had once spoken of him as Irish literature's brightest light.

ALGERNON CHARLES SWINBURNE AND RALPH WALDO EMERSON
This pair were almost permanently at one another's throats.
Swinburne referred to Emerson as a "gap-toothed, hoary-headed
ape," and Emerson retaliated by dubbing Swinburne a leper and
a sodomite. Not to be outdone, Swinburne elaborated by saying
that Emerson was "a wrinkled baboon, a man first hoisted into
notoriety on the shoulders of Carlyle, and who now spits and
sputters on a filthier platform of his own finding and fouling."

SAMUEL BECKETT AND JAMES JOYCE
These two Irish expatriates became close friends in Paris in the
1930s, Beckett acting as Joyce's secretary as well as his friend.
The relationship faltered after Joyce's mentally handicapped
daughter Lucia fell in love with Beckett and Beckett failed to
reciprocate the emotion. One day, Beckett called to see Joyce
and Lucia answered the door. "I'm here to see your father," said
Beckett, "not you." Joyce never forgave him.

NORMAN MAILER AND GORE VIDAL
Mailer and Vidal have been at one another hammer and tongs on
and off for about four decades now, with insults flying back and
forth with such frequency that one almost suspects their ostensible
animosity to have amicable undertones. Mailer once butted Vidal
and has also accused him of everything from narcissism to what
he calls "intellectual pollution." Vidal, on the other hand, sees
Mailer as a sexual fascist obsessed with fame, machismo, and
the cult of personality.

OSCAR WILDE AND GEORGE MOORE
Moore essentially saw Wilde as a plagiarist. "His method of
literary piracy," he said, "was along the lines of the robber
Cacus, who dragged stolen cows backwards by their tails into his
cavern so that their hoofprints might not lead to detection."
Wilde said equally enchantingly of Moore: "He leads his readers

to the latrine and locks them in." Such invective set the stage for years of mutual hostility, so much that one day, when Wilde was asked if he knew Moore, he replied, "Yes indeed. In fact I know him so well I haven't spoken to him for ten years."

WILLIAM FAULKNER AND ERNEST HEMINGWAY
These two drunks had many quarrels about one another's styles. "Hemingway," said Faulkner, "has never been known to use a word that might send a reader to the dictionary." Hemingway countered: "Poor Faulkner. Does he really think big emotions come from big words? I know all the ten-dollar words as well as he does, but I prefer the older, simpler ones."

FYODOR DOSTOEVSKI AND IVAN TURGENEV
The goading between them was both professional and personal. Dostoevski found Turgenev overbearing and lampooned him in print. Turgenev retaliated by dubbing Dostoevski "a pimple on the face of literature."

GEORGE BERNARD SHAW AND OSCAR WILDE
Their rivalry was at a constant simmer. Wilde once said "Shaw hasn't an enemy in the world, and none of his friends like him."

PEN STATE
10 famous fictional places

SHANGRI-LA
The Tibetan retreat where time stands still in James Hilton's 1930s novel *Lost Horizon*.

UTOPIA
Thomas Moore's earthly paradise.

LILLIPUT
The land of the little people in Jonathan Swift's *Gulliver's Travels*.

ELDORADO
The optimists' land of plenty in Voltaire's *Candide*.

EREWHON
Samuel Butler's fictive creation, being (almost) "nowhere" spelled backwards.

SERENDIPITY
Horace Walpole's magic land, where delightful discoveries were made purely by accident.

YOKNAPATAWPHA COUNTY
The fictional setting for most of William Faulkner's novels and stories.

LLAREGGUB
The location of Dylan Thomas' *Under Milk Wood*. It spells "bugger all" backwards.

MIDDLE EARTH
The land of J. R. R. Tolkien's Hobbit-inhabited books.

NARNIA
C. S. Lewis' land through the wardrobe.

CELLULOID SCRIBBLERS
10 movie stars who wrote novels

Simone Signoret *Adieu Volodia*
David Niven *Once Over Lightly*
Jean Harlow *Today is Tonight*
George Kennedy *Murder on Location*
Tony Curtis *Kid Andrew Cody and Julie Sparrow*
Joan Blondell *Center Door Fancy*
Mary Astor *A Place Called Saturday*
Mae West *The Constant Sinner*
Orson Welles *Mr. Arkadin*
Carrie Fisher *Postcards from the Edge*

FROM PENS TO LENS
10 writers who tried their hand at movie direction

James Clavell *To Sir with Love*
Nora Ephron *Sleepless in Seattle*
Norman Mailer *Maidstone*
Tom Stoppard *Rosencrantz and Guildenstern are Dead*
Michael Crichton *Westworld*
Sidney Sheldon *Dream Wife*
Stephen King *Maximum Overdrive*
Samuel Beckett *Film*
Pier Paolo Pasolini *The Gospel According to St. Matthew*
Robert Towne *Personal Best*

FROM PAGE TO CENTER STAGE
5 movies featuring writers in dramatic roles

JAMES DICKEY *Deliverance*
Appears as a sheriff in John Boorman's acclaimed adaptation of his novel.

NORMAN MAILER *Ragtime*
Plays architect Stanford White who is killed by mad millionaire Harry Thaw (Robert Joy) because of a woman.

TRUMAN CAPOTE *Murder By Death*
Capote camps it up as a man who invites the world's greatest detectives (Miss Marple, Sam Spade, Charlie Chan, and Hercule Poirot) to his castle and then informs them they're his prisoners in this offbeat spoof on the gumshoe genre.

MARSHALL MCLUHAN *Annie Hall*
When Woody Allen has words with a guy lining up at a movie theater about what McLuhan's message really is, the man himself appears to tell the guy that he was talking nonsense and that Woody was right. "If only life were like that," opines Woody afterward.

GORE VIDAL *Gattaca*
Vidal is the "who" that "dunit" in this futuristic thriller about a genetically challenged wanna-be with a dream of going into space.

GOOD WILL HUNTING
10 movies based on Shakespeare's plays

West Side Story *Romeo and Juliet*
My Own Private Idaho *Henry IV, Part 1*
Chimes at Midnight *Henry IV, Part 2*
Throne of Blood *Macbeth*
Kiss Me Kate *The Taming of the Shrew*
Carry on Cleo *Antony and Cleopatra*
Forbidden Planet *The Tempest*
An Honorable Murder *Julius Caesar*
A Double Life *Othello*
Joe Macbeth *Macbeth*

TO HAVE AND HAVE NOT
10 financial considerations

W. B. YEATS
When he heard that he had won the Nobel prize in 1923, he said to the man who was enthusiastically giving him the news, "Stop babbling, for God's sake, how much is it worth?"

JONATHAN CAPE
Claimed that the only way publishing paid was if you didn't charge for your time.

LEO TOLSTOY
When, in a burst of geriatric largess (or was it merely fire insurance?), he gave away his worldly possessions to live the life of a simple peasant, his wife Sofya had the good sense to sell the

copyright of his early works to get a few rubles to put bread on the table for herself and her family.

KARL MARX

Marx resigned a journalist post with the *New York Tribune* in the mid-1880s because he felt that he wasn't being paid enough.

SAMUEL TAYLOR COLERIDGE

Had so many money problems as an undergraduate at university that he joined the army under a false name: Silas Tomkyn Comberbache.

J. B. PRIESTLEY

Asked once what he would do if he won £100,000, he replied, "I've got £100,000." The questioner went on to ask, "Yes, but what if you won *another* £100,000?" Priestley replied dryly, "I've *got* another £100,000."

SAMUEL BOYCE

This eighteenth-century Irish poet was so desperate for money, that he used to send his wife out begging for him, advising her to tell people that he was dying so that they might be more generous with their offers.

BRENDAN BEHAN

Was offered £30 for his play *The Twisting of Another Rope* … on condition that the Pike Theatre be allowed to change the name of it. "For thirty quid," Behan replied, "you can change it to *The Brothers Fuckin' Karamazov*."

GEORGE BERNARD SHAW

When movie producer Sam Goldwyn asked him if he would sell him the movie rights to one of his plays, Shaw said to him— with a generous portion of tongue applied to cheek: "The trouble is that you think only of art and I think only of money." When Shaw won the Nobel prize in 1925, he refused the money that accompanied the honor, complaining that he had been besieged with requests for loans from every bankrupt writer he had ever known since it was announced. "I can forgive Alfred Nobel for inventing dynamite," he said, "but only a fiend in human form could have invented the Nobel prize."

SAMUEL JOHNSON
His famous advice was "Anyone who writes for any reason other than money is a blockhead."

PULP PIONEERS
The first 10 paperbacks ever published

The Mysterious Affair at Styles Agatha Christie
The Unpleasantness at the Bellona Club Dorothy L. Sayers
Gone to Earth Mary Webb
Ariel André Maurois
Carnival Compton MacKenzie
A Farewell to Arms Ernest Hemingway
William E. H. Young
Twenty-Five Beverley Nichols
Poet's Pub Eric Linklater
Madame Claire Susan Ertz

British publisher Allen Lane was the pioneer of this cost-effective publishing coup in 1935. He reduced the cost dramatically by printing his "Penguins" on wood-pulp paper and binding the books with paper boards. The first American paperbacks followed four years later in 1939, with Robert DeGraff's Pocket Books. His first titles included Shakespeare and Agatha Christie.

BARBWIRE BOUQUETS
5 quotes on first nights at the theater

"The play was a great success, but the audience a total failure."
>Oscar Wilde after the unsuccessful first night of
>*Lady Windermere's Fan* in 1892

"Well, Mildred, that was the worst play I've seen since *King Lear*."
>Comment overheard after the debut performance of Chekhov's
>*The Cherry Orchard* in Liverpool in 1948

"Your characters talk like typewriting and you yourself talk like a telegram."
>Patrick Campbell's wife to Noël Coward on the first night of his
>play *The Vortex* in 1924

"He delivers every line with a monotonous tenor bark as if addressing an audience of deaf eskimos."
>Michael Billington on Peter O'Toole's version of
>*Macbeth* in 1980

"If I can't go to their openings I'll wait three days and go to their closings."
>Walter Winchell on the works of the Shubert Brothers after they
>banned him from theaters where they were performing

IF YOU CAN'T BEAT THEM ...
5 flagellation freaks

FYODOR DOSTOEVSKI
Got a masochistic thrill from being beaten like a "naughty boy." Sometimes the mere miming of corporal punishment was enough to stimulate him.

T. E. LAWRENCE
Liked to be spanked with a birch rod on his buttocks to the point of seminal emission, and also to be sodomized and kicked with spiked boots during sexual encounters.

ALGERNON CHARLES SWINBURNE
Claimed that his horrific experiences at school left him with an inverted addiction to flagellation. He loved reading de Sade's books and regularly visited a London flogging brothel on Circus Road, St. John's Wood.

JEAN-JACQUES ROUSSEAU
Became fascinated by flagellation after being spanked as a youth by his teacher. When she realized that he was enjoying it, she stopped, but it was too late—he was already addicted.

SAMUEL JOHNSON
Had a lifelong addiction to bondage and flagellation. He kept a set of padlocks and fetters at his home and would engage a friend of his to thrash him repeatedly.

PEN-PALS

10 literary friendships

CHARLES DICKENS AND WILKIE COLLINS
Collins joined Dickens in amateur theatricals after he met him in 1851, and the two of them also collaborated on writing projects.

JAMES BOSWELL AND SAMUEL JOHNSON
Met in a Covent Garden bookshop in 1763 and became great friends. Boswell never really recovered from Johnson's death in 1784. He published his *Life of Samuel Johnson* in 1791.

HERMAN MELVILLE AND NATHANIEL HAWTHORNE
Hawthorne was Melville's best friend and neighbor for some time. He dedicated *Moby Dick* to him.

HILAIRE BELLOC AND G. K. CHESTERTON
This pair were so close, that George Bernard Shaw applied the portmanteau term "Chesterbelloc" to them. Chesterton also illustrated many of Belloc's books.

ERNEST HEMINGWAY AND F. SCOTT FITZGERALD
Fitzgerald was famous first, and gave Hemingway a leg up with his publishers (Scribners). Hemingway's success later outstripped that of Fitzgerald, and the relationship cooled.

W. B. YEATS AND LADY GREGORY
This pair met in 1896. They became firm friends and formed the Irish National Theatre Society five years later, producing plays by each of them and spearheading an Irish literary renaissance in the process.

GUY DE MAUPASSANT AND GUSTAVE FLAUBERT
Flaubert wasn't only Maupassant's friend but his mentor as well, and he sought his views on everything he wrote.

ALEXANDRE DUMAS AND ROGER DE BEAUVOIR
De Beauvoir was a literary friend of Dumas'. Such a friendship was tested to the limits the night Dumas found de Beauvoir in bed with his wife. Instead of throwing him out of the house, he merely said, "It's a cold night. Move over and make room for me."

JAMES JOYCE AND EZRA POUND
This pair became friends when they met in Paris, Pound serializing both *Ulysses* and *Portrait of the Artist* in his magazine the *Egotist*. "He took me out of the gutter," Joyce once said.

RUPERT BROOKE AND VIRGINIA WOOLF
Their platonic relationship was so intimate that they even swam naked together.

GOOD COMPANIONS
55 other literary friendships

William Makepeace Thackeray and Charlotte Brontë
Charles Dickens and Alfred Lord Tennyson
Ralph Waldo Emerson and Algernon Charles Swinburne
Jonathan Swift and Alexander Pope
August Strindberg and Friedrich Nietzsche
Robert Louis Stevenson and Henry James
Edmund Spenser and Sir William Sidney
David Hume and Tobias Smollett
George Bernard Shaw and Thomas Hardy
Sir Walter Scott and David Hume
Arthur Rimbaud and Paul Verlaine
Alexander Pushkin and Nikolai Gogol

Thomas Peacock and Percy Bysshe Shelley
Voltaire and John Gay
George Orwell and Arthur Koestler
Emile Zola and Alphonse Daudet
Jean Racine and Molière
Leo Tolstoy and Ivan Turgenev
John Milton and John Dryden
George Meredith and Dante Gabriel Rossetti
Virginia Woolf and Hugh Walpole
W. Somerset Maugham and H. G. Wells
Christopher Marlowe and Sir Walter Raleigh
Oscar Wilde and Robert Southey
Edward Lear and Alfred Lord Tennyson
T. E. Lawrence and E. M. Forster
D. H. Lawrence and Aldous Huxley
Charles Lamb and William Hazlitt
Rudyard Kipling and Henry James
John Keats and Percy Bysshe Shelley
William Shakespeare and Ben Jonson
Thomas Hardy and Algernon Charles Swinburne
E. M. Forster and Christopher Isherwood
Gustave Flaubert and Victor Hugo
F. Scott Fitzgerald and John Dos Passos
George Eliot and Robert Browning
Arthur Conan Doyle and Jerome K. Jerome
Charles Dickens and William Makepeace Thackeray
William Wordsworth and Thomas De Quincey
Oscar Wilde and Wilkie Collins
Geoffrey Chaucer and John Gower
Lewis Carroll and John Ruskin
Thomas Carlyle and Alfred Lord Tennyson
Lord Byron and Percy Bysshe Shelley

Charlotte Brontë and Elizabeth Gaskell
Robert Browning and Matthew Arnold
Honoré de Balzac and George Sand
Arnold Bennett and H. G. Wells
Jean-Paul Sartre and Simone de Beauvoir
James Joyce and Ernest Hemingway
Allen Ginsberg and Jack Kerouac
T. S. Eliot and Ezra Pound
Jean Cocteau and Jean Genet
James Joyce and Oliver St. John Gogarty
Lord Byron and Thomas Moore

G

CASINO ROYALE

5 writers who had gambling problems

AL ALVAREZ
His obsession with poker is chronicled in *The Biggest Game in Town* (1983).

JOSEPH CONRAD
His gambling debts were so extreme that, in 1878, he tried to shoot himself. The bullet missed his heart, however, and he survived.

FYODOR DOSTOEVSKI
Addicted to roulette and dominoes, he gave them up only when his mountain of debts began to give him nightmares. At its height, his wife was forced to pawn her wedding ring and clothes.

GIACOMO CASANOVA
Loved playing cards for money.

EDGAR WALLACE
His 173 novels earned him a huge fortune, which he blew on gambling and wild living, leaving behind him a string of debts when he died in 1932.

GENDER-BENDERS

10 sex-change pseudonyms

IAIN BLAIR
Better known as bestselling romantic fiction author Emma Blair.

REV. TOBY FORWARD
The vicar who managed, until found out, to convince the women's publisher Virago that he was an Asian woman writer.

MARY ANN EVANS
Took to writing novels at the age of 40 under the pen name of George Eliot.

EMILY, CHARLOTTE, AND ANNE BRONTË
Published respectively under the fraternal names Ellis, Currer, and Acton Bell.

ALEXANDER TROCCHI
The Scots Beat wrote erotica for the Olympia Press in 1950s Paris under the female pseudonym of Frances Lengel.

DOMINIQUE AURY
A case of double bluff. Published the pornographic *Story of O* under the name Pauline Réage, but was widely assumed to have been a man.

AMANDINE DUPIN
This nineteenth-century French novelist wrote under the name of George Sand, inspired by her lover and onetime coauthor Jules Sandeau.

HUGH C. RAE
Two-million-selling Glaswegian author of historical romances who publishes under the name Jessica Stirling.

COLETTE
Her early novels were published by her husband Henri Gaulthier-Villars under his pen name, Willy.

VIOLET MARTIN
Took the pen name Martin Ross for her role in the Irish duo Somerville and Ross, creators of the *Irish RM* trilogy.

GUN CRAZY
5 authors with pistol passion

GRAHAM GREENE
Played Russian roulette at Oxford when he was feeling depressed.

WILLIAM S. BURROUGHS
Killed his partner Joan while trying to shoot a glass from the top of her head in Mexico City in 1951.

ALFRED JARRY
Would spend his days drunk wandering Paris, dressed in cycling garb, and carrying his two pistols, with which he'd threaten bystanders.

ERNEST HEMINGWAY
A man who'd prized guns all his life, he used one to blow the top of his head off while suffering from depression in 1961.

MAXIM GORKI
Tried to shoot himself in the heart when he was 19. He missed, the bullet lodged in his lung, and he survived.

H

BUM DEAL

10 writers who suffered from hemorrhoids

Percy Bysshe Shelley
Edgar Allan Poe
Gerard Manley Hopkins
Alexander Pope
Thomas De Quincey
Lytton Strachey
Charles Dickens
Martin Luther
Fyodor Dostoevski
Nikolai Gogol

THE DOORS OF PERCEPTION

5 writers who hallucinated

VIRGINIA WOOLF
Hallucinated and heard voices at moments of high nervous trauma.

GUY DE MAUPASSANT
Hallucinated as a result of the syphilis that finally killed him.

WILLIAM BLAKE
Was often visited by inspiring visions from the spiritual world.

JOHN RUSKIN
Suffered from manic depression and often saw visions.

HANS CHRISTIAN ANDERSEN
Would hallucinate after nightmares brought on by his hypochondria.

PLAY PENS
60 authors' hobbies

George Bernard Shaw (Singing)
Hilaire Belloc (Sailing)
Dermot Bolger (Soccer)
Arnold Bennett (Calligraphy)
James Boswell (Singing)
Elizabeth Barrett Browning (Riding)
Sir Richard Burton (Falconry)
Lord Byron (Swimming)
Lewis Carroll (Photography)
Oliver Goldsmith (Flute playing)
Samuel Beckett (Chess)
James Joyce (Singing)
Brendan Behan (Swimming)
Charles Baudelaire (Dancing)
J. M. Barrie (Cricket)
Honoré de Balzac (Hypnotism)
Jane Austen (Embroidery)
Matthew Arnold (Ice-skating)
August Strindberg (Fencing)
Vladimir Nabokov (Butterfly collecting)
Alexander Pushkin (Gambling)
Mark Twain (Billiards)
Anthony Trollope (Hunting)
Arthur Rimbaud (Piano)
Jean-Jacques Rousseau (Gardening)
Alfred Lord Tennyson (Yachting)
P. G. Wodehouse (Golf)
William Wordsworth (Dancing)

Percy Bysshe Shelley (Sailing)
W. B. Yeats (Astrology)
R. B. Sheridan (Gambling)
John Milton (Fencing)
T. E. Lawrence (Gymnastics)
Edgar Allan Poe (Swimming)
George Meredith (Piano playing)
Guy de Maupassant (Rowing)
W. Somerset Maugham (Croquet)
Andrew Marvell (Fencing)
D. H. Lawrence (Painting)
Johann Goethe (Botany)
Thomas Hardy (Cycling)
Ernest Hemingway (Hunting)
Victor Hugo (Art)
Henrik Ibsen (Fishing)
Samuel Johnson (Rowing)
John Keats (Cricket)
Friedrich Nietzsche (Riding)
Rudyard Kipling (Golf)
Alexander Pope (Gardening)
Anton Chekhov (Fishing)
Samuel Taylor Coleridge (Horticulture)
Wilkie Collins (Sailing)
Joseph Conrad (Card playing)
William Cowper (Cricket)
Charles Dickens (Hypnotism and conjuring)
Arthur Conan Doyle (Cricket)
John Dryden (Bowls)
George Eliot (Tennis)
E. M. Forster (Piano)
Gustave Flaubert (Canoeing)

ALL IN THE MIND
5 writers who were hypochondriacs

SAMUEL JOHNSON
Lived in terror that one day he would go mad.

JONATHAN SWIFT
Like Johnson, Swift worried more about his mental than his physical health, and always feared that he would decay "like a tree, from the top first." Indeed this was exactly what happened, as he developed aphasia toward the end of his life. He also suffered from Ménière's syndrome.

MARCEL PROUST
His fear of developing diseases from germs was so intense that if he dropped a pen on the floor he refused to pick it up.

PERCY BYSSHE SHELLEY
Once feared he had elephantiasis, a disease consisting of the overgrowth of the skin and connective tissue.

HANS CHRISTIAN ANDERSEN
Was so frightened of being burned to death that, whenever he was in a strange house, he carried a piece of rope with him so that he could slide to safety if he was sleeping in an upstairs room. He was also terrified of being buried alive and asked that, after his death, one of his arteries be cut before he was put into the coffin.

I

WILD OATS
5 writers who had illegitimate children

ROBERT BURNS
His wife brought up one of his illegitimate children as part of the family.

WILKIE COLLINS
Had three illegitimate children by one woman, while he lived with another. Remained a bachelor all his life.

ALEXANDRE DUMAS
Professed to have had dozens of illegitimate children, but acknowledged only three of them.

WILLIAM WORDSWORTH
Had an illegitimate child by Annette Vallon, with whom he had an affair while he was in Paris shortly after the French Revolution.

DANIEL DEFOE
Had an illegitimate son, Benjamin, by an oyster seller.

SIBLING RIBALDRY
5 writers who had incestuous relationships

FRIEDRICH NIETZSCHE
His sister crawled into bed with him on the night their baby brother died—thus began a series of sexual encounters that wracked him with guilt, but which he was unable to resist.

LORD BYRON
Seduced his married half sister Augusta Leigh in 1813, which resulted in the birth of a baby girl, Medora.

GIACOMO CASANOVA
Had sexual relations with his daughter Leonilda, which resulted in the birth of a baby boy. Casanova commented afterward, "I have never been able to understand how a father could tenderly love his charming daughter without having slept with her at least once." In fact, he nearly married his own daughter, but the girl's mother appeared in the church just in time.

VOLTAIRE
Had an incestuous relationship with his niece, Marie-Louise Deis.

COLETTE
Rumored to have been incestuous with her stepson, Bertrand de Jouvenel.

MEN (AND WOMEN) OF LETTERS
40 names behind the initials

D. M. Thomas (Donald Mitchell)
C. V. Wedgwood (Cicely Veronica)
A. S. Byatt (Antonia Susan)
M. R. James (Montague Rhodes)
P. D. James (Phyllis Dorothy)
C. S. Forester (Cecil Scott)
R. P. Blackmur (Richard Palmer)
P. G. Wodehouse (Pelham Grenville)
H. G. Wells (Herbert George)

C. S. Lewis (Clive Staples)
D. H. Lawrence (David Herbert)
J. M. Barrie (James Matthew)
J. P. Donleavy (James Patrick)
A. J. Cronin (Archibald Joseph)
E. L. Doctorow (Edgar Lawrence)
V. S. Pritchett (Victor Sawdon)
J. B. Priestley (John Boynton)
R. D. Laing (Ronald David)
D. J. Enright (Denis Joseph)
E. M. Forster (Edward Morgan)
J. D. Salinger (Jerome David)
W. H. Auden (Wystan Hugh)
e. e. cummings (edward estlin)
J. G. Ballard (James Graham)
P. J. O'Rourke (Patrick Jake)
T. S. Eliot (Thomas Stearns)
G. K. Chesterton (Gilbert Keith)
C. P. Snow (Charles Percy)
L. P. Hartley (Leslie Poles)
H. L. Mencken (Henry Louis)
T. H. White (Terence Hanbury)
F. Scott Fitzgerald (Francis)
Hunter S. Thompson (Stockton)
George S. Kaufman (Simon)
Jerome K. Jerome (Klapka)
William S. Burroughs (Seward)
Arthur C. Clarke (Charles)
James M. Cain (Mallahan)
J. R. R. Tolkien (John Ronald Reuel)
Pearl S. Buck (Sydenstricker)

CERTIFIED

10 writers who went insane

JOHN RUSKIN
Suffered intermittently from mental illness throughout his life, and finally went mad while lecturing at Oxford, when he had to be dragged screaming from the podium.

EZRA POUND
Judged to be of unsound mind in 1946 after being convicted of treason for pro-Hitler propagandizing in the same year. He went on to spend thirteen years incarcerated in an asylum.

GUY DE MAUPASSANT
Died in a lunatic asylum at the age of 42, having been tipped over the edge by the syphilis that plagued him for most of his life.

FRIEDRICH NIETZSCHE
Had always been a loose cannon throughout his turbulent life, but excelled even himself one day in 1889, when he saw a horse on the street being mistreated by its master and broke down in tears, throwing his arms round the horse as if it were a lover. Thus began a period of psychological disintegration that saw him spend the last eleven years of his life in an asylum.

JONATHAN SWIFT
Committed to the care of guardians in 1742, when he lost his mind. In his will, rather fittingly, he left £8,000 for the erection of a mental home in Dublin. The instruction came with this characteristic epithet:

> *He gave what little wealth he had*
> *To build a house for fools and mad*
> *And showed by one satiric touch*
> *No nation wanted it so much!*

JOHN CLARE

Taken to Northampton General Lunatic Asylum in 1841 and remained there until his death twenty-three years later. He was free to go into town, where he would scribble verse on scraps of paper for the townsfolk.

CHARLES LAMB

Suffered a bout of madness in 1796 and, writing to his friend Coleridge, said, "The six weeks that finished last year and began this, your very humble servant spent very agreeably in a mad house at Hoxton—I am got somewhat rational now and don't bite anymore."

ANTONIN ARTAUD

A manic depressive; after an incident of mania on a ship sailing between Ireland and France in 1937, he was put in a straitjacket at Le Havre and was incarcerated until his death in 1946.

FREDERICK EXLEY

Troubled by bouts of insanity, which led to regular incarceration, as chronicled in his autobiographical fiction.

WILLIAM COWPER

Suffered regular bouts of mental instability. Hearing voices that told him to kill himself, he tried to commit suicide in 1763.

NIGHTHAWKS

10 writers who suffered from insomnia

Joseph Conrad
J. M. Barrie
Marcel Proust

Alexander Pope
Arnold Bennett
Hilaire Belloc
Charles Dickens
Alexandre Dumas
R. B. Sheridan
Rudyard Kipling

99% PERSPIRATION
10 authors' inspirations

RAYMOND CHANDLER
Was best inspired to write by watching his wife doing the house-work in the nude.

AGATHA CHRISTIE
Said she got some of her best ideas while washing the dishes.

EDNA O'BRIEN
Claims that she always works best after having a cup of tea.

GORE VIDAL
"First coffee, then a bowel movement, and then the muse joins me."

F. SCOTT FITZGERALD
Generally needed alcohol to summon his muse: "Any stories I wrote when I was sober," he once said, "were stupid."

GEORGE BERNARD SHAW
Said the main reason he became a writer was because an author need not dress respectably, "since he's never seen by his clients, as is the case with other professions."

D. H. LAWRENCE
Enjoyed writing when he felt spiteful. "It's like having a good sneeze," he used to say.

HEINRICH HEINE
Kept a picture of his friend and mentor, August Strindberg, on his desk to awaken his muse.

KINGSLEY AMIS
Once claimed that his main motivation to write came from the urge to annoy his readers.

GRAHAM GREENE
Said he wrote primarily because he didn't like himself and his characters provided an escape from his own identity.

SHOOTING FROM THE LIP
20 writers insulting other writers

"The more I read him, the less I wonder why they poisoned him."
Thomas Babington Macaulay on Socrates

"He's able to turn an unplotted, unworkable manuscript into an unworkable, unplotted manuscript with a lot of sex."
Tom Volpe on Harold Robbins

"I remember coming across George Bernard Shaw at the Grand Canyon and finding him refusing to admire it. He was jealous!"
J. B. Priestley

"I cannot abide his souvenir-shop style, bottled ships and shell necklaces of romantic clichés."

Vladimir Nabokov on Joseph Conrad

"I think Norman Mailer is our greatest writer. What's unfortunate is that our greatest writer should be a bum."

Pauline Kael

"Swinburne stands up to his neck in a cesspool, and then adds to its contents."

Thomas Carlyle

"A queasy undergraduate scratching his pimples."

Virginia Woolf on James Joyce

"Under the dirty clumsy paws of a harper whose plectrum is a muckrake, any tune will become a chaos of discords."

Algernon Charles Swinburne on Walt Whitman

"George Moore wrote excellent poetry until he discovered grammar."

Oscar Wilde

"That garden gnome expelled from Eden has come to rest as a gargoyle brooding over a derelict cathedral."

Kenneth Tynan on Malcolm Muggeridge

"Some people kiss and tell. George Moore told but did not kiss."

Susan Mitchell

"Henry James had a sensibility so fine, no mere idea could ever penetrate it."

T. S. Eliot

"He couldn't blow his nose without moralizing on the conditions in the handkerchief industry."

Cyril Connolly on George Orwell

"Alexander Solzhenitsyn is a bad novelist and a fool. The combination usually makes for great popularity in the U.S."

Gore Vidal

"Tennyson is a beautiful half of a poet."

Ralph Waldo Emerson

"Henry James writes fiction as if it were a painful duty."

Oscar Wilde

"Shaw writes like a Pakistani who learned English when he was 12 in order to become a chartered accountant."

John Osborne

"Poor Matt. He's gone to heaven, no doubt—but he won't like God."

Robert Louis Stevenson on the demise of Matthew Arnold

"Heinrich Heine so loosened the corsets of the German language that today every little salesman can fondle her breasts."

Karl Kraus

"Every word Lillian Hellman wrote was a lie—including 'and' and 'the'."

Mary McCarthy

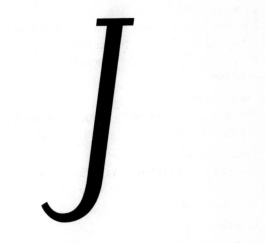

INSIDE STORIES
20 writers who went to jail

BRENDAN BEHAN
Sentenced to three years in Borstal for an IRA bombing campaign in England in 1939, and a further fourteen for trying to kill a detective in 1942. The latter sentence was dramatically reduced in an amnesty.

THOMAS PAINE
Though a supporter of the Revolution, he was jailed by Robespierre in 1794 for opposing the execution of the king.

VACLAV HAVEL
The dramatist and subsequent Czech president was jailed by the communist authorities for four and a half years in 1979 for his subversive activities.

JEAN GENET
Spent many years of his life in prison (for picking pockets, male prostitution, and vagrancy), where he began to write while serving a life sentence after ten convictions for theft.

JOHN BUNYAN
Spent twelve years in prison for preaching Christian beliefs which didn't conform to those of the established church of the day.

ROBERT LEIGHTON
This Scottish mystic wrote *Synon's Plea Against Prelacy* in 1630. The ecclesiastical establishment was so upset by it that he was imprisoned, whipped, his ears cut off, and his nose slit. In addition, the letters "SS," standing for "Sower of Sedition," were branded onto his face.

BEN JONSON
Was imprisoned for killing a fellow actor in a duel and for libeling the Scots in his play *Eastward Ho* in 1605.

GABRIELE D'ANNUNZIO
Sentenced to five months in prison in 1891 for having an affair with the wife of a Neapolitan nobleman.

MARQUIS DE SADE
Imprisoned for twelve years in 1777 after being accused of trying to sodomize and poison five Marseilles prostitutes.

PAUL VERLAINE
Served eighteen months for assaulting his gay lover Arthur Rimbaud, and a further two years for trying to stab him to death on another occasion.

NORMAN MAILER
Arrested for civil disobedience during the march on the Pentagon on October 21, 1967 in which he protested vociferously (and also drunkenly) against the Vietnam War. He was sentenced to thirty days' imprisonment but this was suspended after a bail bond of $500 was put up for him. He ended up spending just one night in jail. He records it all in *Armies of the Night*.

EMILE ZOLA
Spent a year in the clink after insisting that the government fabricated evidence against a Jewish military officer, Captain Dreyfus, with his famous "J'Accuse" letter.

OSCAR WILDE
Spent two years in Reading Jail after losing his libel suit against the Marquess of Queensbury and being convicted of homosexuality.

O. HENRY
Served three years in a federal penitentiary in Ohio in 1905 for embezzling funds while working as a bank teller.

HONORÉ DE BALZAC
Was once imprisoned for a week for failing to perform guard duty in the national service.

FYODOR DOSTOEVSKI
Served four years' hard labor as a political prisoner in Siberia. At one point, he was actually sentenced to death, being blindfolded and tied to a post as a firing squad took aim, but the sentence was commuted at the very last moment.

SIR THOMAS MALORY
Was put in prison no fewer than eight times for crimes including rape and armed robbery.

KEN KESEY
Jailed in 1967 for possession of marijuana. Before standing trial, he fled to Mexico and unsuccessfully tried to fake his suicide.

JACK LONDON
Arrested for vagrancy when sleeping rough near Niagara Falls in 1894. He was deloused, given thirty days' hard labor, handcuffed to a chain gang, and put to work under the scrutiny of a group of guards armed with Winchesters. The filth and degradation he witnessed haunted him for the rest of his life.

JOE ORTON
Jailed for six months for defacing library books.

MID-SENTENCE

10 books written while the authors were in jail

MIGUEL CERVANTES
Wrote *Don Quixote* in Seville Prison after being jailed for debt in 1597.

SIR WALTER RALEIGH
Wrote *History of the World* in the Tower of London, where he was sentenced to death in 1603 on a trumped-up charge of treason against King James. He was reprieved and released on parole, but recaptured two years later and executed for the same charge in 1618.

BOETHIUS
Wrote his most famous work, *The Consolation of Philosophy*, while imprisoned at Pavia in 524, awaiting execution.

JOHN CLELAND
Wrote *Fanny Hill* in Newgate Prison, where he was incarcerated for debt. Remuneration from the sale of the novel eventually secured his release.

OSCAR WILDE
There's a common misconception that Wilde wrote *The Ballad of Reading Gaol* during his imprisonment. In fact, it was written after his release. The jail book was *De Profundis*.

BERTRAND RUSSELL
Wrote *An Introduction to Mathematical Philosophy* when in jail in London during World War I for being a conscientious objector.

ADOLF HITLER

Dictated the first part of *Mein Kampf* to his disciple Rudolf Hess in 1923, when in jail in Germany after an unsuccessful bid to seize power.

O. HENRY

Wrote his short-story collection *The Gentle Grafter* while serving a three-year sentence in 1905.

RICHARD LOVELACE

During his first stint in prison in 1642, he wrote his extended poem *To Althea*; his second stint, six years later, yielded *To Lucasta, Going to the Wars*.

JOHN BUNYAN

Bunyan was also imprisoned twice—for unlicensed preaching. During his first spell, which lasted twelve years, he wrote his autobiography *Grace Abounding* (in 1666). During his second spell, eleven years on, he started his most famous book, *Pilgrim's Progress*.

HACKED TO BITS
5 writers on journalism

"The newspaper is the natural enemy of the book as the whore is of the decent woman."

Edmund de Goncourt

"Once a newspaper touches a story, the facts are lost forever, even to the protagonists."

Norman Mailer

"Journalism is the last refuge of the literary mediocre."

Brendan Behan

"If an editor can only make people angry enough, they will write half his newspaper for him for nothing."

G. K. Chesterton

"It is inexcusable for scientists to torture animals. Let them do their experiments on journalists instead."

Henrik Ibsen

K

ARISE

10 authors who were knighted

Kingsley Amis
Richard Burton
Arthur Conan Doyle
P. G. Wodehouse
J. M. Barrie
Osbert Sitwell
Noel Coward
Compton MacKenzie
Hugh Walpole
Terence Rattigan

SHUFFLING OFF
30 authors' famous last words

FRANÇOIS RABELAIS
"I am going to seek the Great Perhaps."

JAMES THURBER
"God bless, God damn."

DAMON RUNYON
"You can keep the things of bronze and stone and give me just one man to remember me once a year."

W. SOMERSET MAUGHAM
"Dying is a dull, dreary affair. My advice to you is to have nothing whatsoever to do with it."

R. B. SHERIDAN
"I am absolutely undone and broken-hearted."

NOEL COWARD
"Goodnight my darlings, I'll see you tomorrow."

LYTTON STRACHEY
"If this is dying, I don't think much of it."

HENRY JAMES
"So it has come at last, the distinguished thing."

WILLIAM SAROYAN
"Everybody's got to die, but I always thought an exception would be made in my case. Now what?"

HEINRICH HEINE
"God will forgive me; that's His trade."

DYLAN THOMAS
"I've had 18 straight whiskeys. I think that's the record."

ANTON CHEKHOV
"It's a long time since I've drunk champagne."

D.H. LAWRENCE
"I'm getting better."

HENRIK IBSEN
"On the contrary." (After his wife suggested he was looking better.)

JOHANN GOETHE
"Open the second shutter so more light can come in."

GIACOMO CASANOVA
"I have lived as a philosopher but I'll die a Christian."

TOBIAS SMOLLETT
"All is well, my dear."

ALEXANDER POPE
"Here I am, dying of a hundred good symptoms." (After the doctor said he was looking well.)

LEO TOLSTOY
"Even in the valley of the shadow of death, two and two do not make six." (Refusing to return to the Orthodox Church that had once excommunicated him.)

VICTOR HUGO
"I see a black light."

GEORGE BERNARD SHAW
"Sister, you are trying to keep me alive as an old curiosity, but I'm done, I'm finished." (To his nurse, Gwendoline Howell.)

SIR WALTER RALEIGH
"It is a sharp remedy, but a sure one for all ills." (Spoken from the scaffold before he was decapitated.)

VIRGINIA WOOLF
"I have a feeling I shall go mad. I cannot go on any longer in these terrible times." (Spoken before her suicide.)

D. H. LAWRENCE
"It's time for morphine."

ALEXANDRE DUMAS
"I shall never know how it all comes out now." (Referring to his unfinished *Count of Monte Cristo*.)

H. L. MENCKEN
"Tell my friends I'm in a hell of a mess."

OSCAR WILDE
"Either that wallpaper goes or I do."

JAMES JOYCE
"Is there one who understands me?"

FRANK O'CONNOR
"I hope you don't expect me to entertain you."

BRENDAN BEHAN
"Thank you, sister. May you be the mother of a bishop!"

THE LONG ARM OF THE LAW
10 writers who were lawyers

John Mortimer
Scott Turow
Robert Louis Stevenson
La Fontaine
Nathalie Sarraute
Wallace Stevens
John Grisham
Louis Auchincloss
Joseph Sheridan Le Fanu
Earle Stanley Gardner

FATHERS IN LAW
15 writers whose fathers were lawmen

Hilaire Belloc
John Millington Synge
Elizabeth Bowen
P. G. Wodehouse
William Wordsworth
Sir Walter Scott
Anthony Trollope
François Rabelais
W. Somerset Maugham
Johann Goethe

C. S. Lewis
James Dickey
Margaret Mitchell
Jorge Luis Borges
Simone de Beauvoir

THE LAW'S DELAY
5 writers who studied law but didn't make a career of it

JAMES BOSWELL
Began practicing in Edinburgh in 1766 but his preference for writing soon took over.

HONORÉ DE BALZAC
Completed law studies at the Sorbonne and worked for three years as a law clerk before going into writing full time.

ALEXANDRE DUMAS
Did a brief stint as a solicitor's clerk, but left to work for the Duc d'Orleans, who went on to become King Louis Philippe.

WILKIE COLLINS
Called to the bar in 1851, but he never practiced.

ARNOLD BENNETT
His father was a solicitor and wanted him to carry on the tradition, but he continued to fail his legal exams and after a short spell as a legal clerk he went into journalism.

RED LETTER DAYS
5 epistolary anecdotes

VOLTAIRE
After receiving an abusive letter from a rival, Voltaire retorted: "I am sitting in the smallest room in the house with your missive before me. It will shortly be behind me."

HERBERT BEERBOHM TREE
Sent this note to a would-be writer: "My dear Sir, I have read your play. Oh, my dear Sir!"

SAMUEL JOHNSON
Johnson once received an unsolicited offering which didn't impress him. He sent this reply: "Sir, Your manuscript is both good and original. But the part that is good is not original, and the part that is original is not good."

VICTOR HUGO
The shortest correspondence on record is that between Hugo and his publisher in 1862. He was on vacation and wrote to ask how his latest novel (*Les Misérables*) was selling. He made just one stroke of the pen—a question mark—and received just one in return—an exclamation mark. *Touché!*

NOEL COWARD
When T. E. Lawrence was in the RAF, Coward wrote him a letter beginning, "Dear 338171. May I call you 338?"

SHELF LIFE
5 writers who were librarians

AUGUST STRINDBERG
Worked at the Royal Library of Stockholm from 1874 to 1882.

FRANK O'CONNOR
Took the Republican side in the Irish Civil War and was interned when it finished in 1923. Upon his release, he joined the library service.

PHILIP LARKIN
Librarian at the Brynmor Jones Library at the University of Hull from 1955 until his death thirty years later.

GIACOMO CASANOVA
After a life of orgiastic abandon, Casanova ended his days as a librarian to a count in Bohemia.

JORGE LUIS BORGES
Became director of the National Library of Argentina in 1955 when Peron fell from power. Held the post until his retirement in 1975.

TIME TO GO?
5 authors who enjoyed longevity

BENJAMIN FRANKLIN
Helped to write the United States Constitution at 81.

W. SOMERSET MAUGHAM
Wrote *Points of View* at the age of 84.

JOHANN GOETHE
Finished *Faust* when he was 81.

WINSTON CHURCHILL
Wrote *A History of the English Speaking People* at 82.

LEO TOLSTOY
Wrote the appropriately titled *I Cannot Be Silent* at 82.

DEAD LOSSES
10 lost manuscripts

ALBERT CAMUS
The manuscript of *The First Man* was found in the wreckage of
the automobile in which he was killed in 1960, but it wasn't
published until 1994.

MALCOLM LOWRY
In 1932, a publisher who was considering Lowry's manuscript of
Ultramarine left it in his car to make a phone call and when he
came back it was gone. He offered to pay Lowry a handsome fee
to rewrite it but luckily one of Lowry's friends managed to unearth
some copies of the work in progress from a wastepaper basket.

JOHN STEINBECK
An early draft of his *Of Mice and Men* was destroyed when his
setter pup chewed it to bits. He later commended his canine
friend for judicious critical judgment.

ARTHUR CONAN DOYLE
Doyle was similarly relieved when his first novel, *The Narrative
of John Smith*, got lost in the mail, because in hindsight he
realized that it contained much libelous content.

DANTE GABRIEL ROSSETTI

Overcome with grief at the death of his wife from an overdose of laudanum, he placed the only copy of his poems in her coffin when she was buried. Seven years later, however, he claimed that her spirit came to him in the form of a chaffinch and told him to reclaim them, which he duly did after having her dug up.

ERNEST HEMINGWAY

Virtually all of his early stories and a novel in progress were stolen from a train in Paris when his first wife Hadley, who was bringing them to him in Lausanne, left her seat to get a drink.

ALFRED LORD TENNYSON

Tennyson lost the text of *Poems Wholly Lyrical* through his own fault and had to start the composition again from scratch.

T. E. LAWRENCE

Lost the manuscript of *The Seven Pillars of Wisdom* at a train station in 1919 while changing trains. He rewrote it from his preliminary notes and it went on to become a runaway bestseller.

SOPHOCLES

Wrote more than a hundred plays, but only seven have survived.

JEAN GENET

Started writing *Our Lady of the Flowers* in prison. The manuscript was discovered and destroyed. Genet rewrote it from memory and had it smuggled safely out of his cell.

THE OBJECT OF MY AFFECTION
15 writers on love

"Scratch a lover and find a foe."

Dorothy Parker

"Love never dies of starvation, but often of indigestion."

Ninon de Lenclos

"Love is the history of a woman's life; it is an episode in a man's."

Madame de Stael

"Of course it's possible to love a human being—if you don't know them too well."

Charles Bukowski

"What better proof can there be of love than money?"

Quentin Crisp

"Love is a fan club with only two fans."

Adrian Henri

"I can understand companionship. I can understand bought sex in the afternoon. I cannot understand the love affair."

Gore Vidal

"Love is blind, but marriage restores its sight."

G. C. Lichtenberg

"Love seeks not to possess, but to be possessed."

R. H. Benson

"I love her and she loves me, and we hate each other with a mild hatred born of love."

August Strindberg

"The fickleness of the woman I love is equaled by the infernal constancy of the woman who loves me."

George Bernard Shaw

"To fall in love is to create a religion that has a fallible God."

Jorge Luis Borges

"No woman is worth more than a fiver unless you're in love with her."

W. Somerset Maugham

"To fall in love you have to be in the state of mind for it to take —like a disease."

Nancy Mitford

"This thing called love. There's none of it, you know. There's only fucking."

Samuel Beckett

M

FOR BETTER OR WORSE

15 writers on wedlock

"Marriage: six weeks of flames and thirty years of ashes."

Giuseppe de Lampedusa

"I only regret one of my marriages. After the ceremony I went to a bar and when the barman asked me what I wanted to drink, I said 'Hemlock'."

Ernest Hemingway

"Staying married may have long-term benefits. You can elicit much more sympathy over a bad marriage than you ever can from a good divorce."

P. J. O'Rourke

"They dream in courtship, but in wedlock wake."

Alexander Pope

"It is a woman's business to get married as soon as possible, and a man's to keep unmarried as long as he can."

George Bernard Shaw

"Whenever a husband and wife begin to discuss their marriage, they are giving evidence at an inquest."

H. L. Mencken

"After a few years of marriage a man can look right at a woman without seeing her, and a woman can see right through a man without looking at him."

Helen Rowland

"Many a man in love with a dimple makes the mistake of marrying the whole girl."

Stephen Leacock

"A man's friends like him but leave him as he is. His wife loves him and is always trying to turn him into somebody else."

G. K. Chesterton

"Every woman should marry an archaeologist, because to him she grows increasingly attractive as she grows older."

Agatha Christie

"The one charm of marriage is that it makes a life of deception absolutely necessary to both parties."

Oscar Wilde

"Most marriages don't add two people together: they subtract one from the other."

Ian Fleming

"The dread of loneliness is greater than the fear of bondage, so we get married."

Cyril Connolly

"If people waited to know each other before they married, the world wouldn't be so over-populated as it is now."

W. Somerset Maugham

"Marriage isn't a process of prolonging the life of love, but of mummifying the corpse."

P. G. Wodehouse

BOOKBINDING
10 literary marriages

Robert Browning and Elizabeth Barrett Browning
Joan Didion and John Gregory Dunne

Colette and Henri Gaulthier-Villars
Ernest Hemingway and Martha Gellhorn
Mary Shelley and Percy Bysshe Shelley
Ted Hughes and Sylvia Plath
Robert Lowell and Elizabeth Hardwick
Mary McCarthy and Edmund Wilson
Raymond Carver and Tess Gallagher
Paul and Jane Bowles

THE MOURNING AFTER THE KNOT BEFORE

10 unusual marriages

AL ALVAREZ

Alvarez realized that his marriage might be in trouble when, the morning after the first night with his new bride, he brought her her breakfast in bed and she looked at it in dismay saying, "The crusts. You didn't cut off the crusts."

JOHN RUSKIN

Found the sight of his wife's pubic hair so disgusting on their wedding night that he resolved never to sleep with her again.

DOROTHY PARKER

Parker remarried her ex-hubby Alan Parker after they'd been divorced three years. When somebody at the wedding reception commented that some of the people present hadn't spoken to one another for years, Dorothy quipped, "Including the bride and groom!"

AUGUST STRINDBERG

On his wedding night, Strindberg tried to strangle his wife. After she struggled free, he explained to her that he had had a nightmare and imagined she was his previous wife.

THOMAS CARLYLE

When it was suggested to Alfred Lord Tennyson that the marriage of Thomas and Jane Carlyle was a mistake because they were unhappy, he replied, "I totally disagree. By any other arrangement, four people would have been unhappy instead of two."

PERCY BYSSHE SHELLEY

On Shelley"s wedding night, the landlord of the inn where he was spending the night banged on his door in the wee small hours and told him that it was customary in Edinburgh (where the inn was situated) for the guests to come in and wash the bride with whiskey. Shelley was not impressed.

JOHN MILTON

His marriage to 17-year-old Mary Powell lasted just one month. She refused to return to him after a visit to her family home. Shortly afterward he became a controversial advocate of divorce.

KATHERINE MANSFIELD

Left her husband on their wedding day and ran off with her childhood sweetheart.

W. H. AUDEN

Auden was gay, but in 1936 he married Erika Mann, the daughter of Thomas, so that she could get a British passport. They met for the first time on their wedding day.

CORNELL WOOLRICH

This hard-boiled oddball married while writing for the Hollywood studios, but the marriage was never consummated and he returned to live with his mother until her death.

ONE IS NOT ENOUGH
5 extramarital scribes

PERCY BYSSHE SHELLEY
Spent three years in a *ménage à trois* with his wife Mary and mistress Claire Clairmont.

JAMES JOYCE
Once asked his wife Nora to sleep with other men to give him fodder for his writing.

EMILE ZOLA
Had two separate families by his wife and mistress and lived with both alternately.

H. G. WELLS
Once performed the unusual act of trying to commit adultery with his own wife. It happened when he was denied sex by his second wife and ran back to his first one, begging her to sleep with him. (She said no.) In later times, he moved his first wife in with his second one while he continued to see his mistress!

GABRIELLE D'ANNUNZIO
When he found out that his wife was pregnant by another man shortly after he married her, he became unfaithful to her, and thus began a spree of adultery.

BACHELORS OF ARTS

10 writers who never married

RUPERT BROOKE
His ideal of female perfection was too high, and was never personified by any one woman enough to persuade him to go to the altar.

GUSTAVE FLAUBERT
Never married because he felt no woman could mean as much to him as his mother, who lived with him until her death.

ANDREW MARVELL
He never married, but after he died, his housekeeper Mary Palmer tried to pass herself off as his widow so that she could inherit his money.

EMILY DICKINSON
Was usually happier with her own company than that of anyone else, but she did form strong friendships, and at the age of 48 she had a romance with a 64-year-old widower.

WILKIE COLLINS
Though he never married, he lived with Caroline Graves for forty years.

ALEXANDER POPE
Wanted to marry Martha Blount, but she didn't reciprocate his feelings, so he remained a bachelor.

OLIVER GOLDSMITH
Suffered the same fate, with a woman called Mary Horneck.

EDWARD LEAR
Was turned off the idea of going to the altar when his affair with Augusta Bethell fell apart.

LEWIS CARROLL
Was a fellow of Christ Church, Oxford, and one of its provisos was for its members to remain single. (Some accounts of his life conflict with this evaluation of his marital ambitions, claiming that he proposed to Alice Liddell but was rebuffed.)

VOLTAIRE
Felt that marriage would interfere with his (fairly hectic) sex life.

PORTNOY'S COMPLAINT
10 writers who masturbated

ANDRÉ GIDE
Expelled from school for doing it in class at the age of 11. (His doctor subsequently threatened to castrate him if he didn't give up.)

SAMUEL PEPYS
Liked to masturbate while reading pornography … and then record the experience in coded form in his diaries.

EDWARD LEAR
Was addicted to the habit in youth, and ascribed both his depression and epilepsy to it.

YUKIO MISHIMA
Practiced it frequently throughout his life, both between and during romances with women. In fact, he once defined *seppuku*, the ritual suicide by which he would eventually die, as "the ultimate form of masturbation."

GUY DE MAUPASSANT
Addicted to it in his early teens, but then was inducted into the charms of womenfolk and decided that this was more fun by far.

PATRICK KAVANAGH
Said he gave up the habit when women entered his life, but the fact that he had the main character in *The Great Hunger*, his most famous poem, indulging in it was difficult to live down.

JAMES BOSWELL
Was so plagued with guilt over it as a young teenager that he considered castrating himself.

TRUMAN CAPOTE
Said the thing he liked most about it was that you didn't have to take your hand to dinner afterward.

HAROLD ROBBINS
Described it as the second most enjoyable thing you could do on your own. (The first was writing.)

JAMES JOYCE
Wracked with guilt about it when he was young, but after he married Nora he gleefully discussed the topic with her and even gave her tips about how best to go about it. (One day, when a fan of his writing said to him, "Let me shake the hand that wrote *Ulysses*," he replied, "No—it's done lots of other things, too!")

DOCTORED SPIRITS
15 writers who held down medical jobs

Ken Kesey (Aide on the psychiatric ward of a hospital)
Colleen McCullough (Neurophysiologist)
Arthur Conan Doyle (Eye doctor)
William Carlos Williams (Pediatrician)

Agatha Christie (Nurse)
Anton Chekhov (Doctor)
François Rabelais (Doctor)
Oliver Goldsmith (Physician)
Bertolt Brecht (Hospital orderly)
John Keats (Apothecary)
A. J. Cronin (Doctor)
James Herriott (Veterinarian)
Robert Bridges (Physician)
Céline (Doctor)
Tobias Smollett (Naval surgeon)

WHEN THE SWORD IS MIGHTIER THAN THE PEN

20 writers with military experience

J.D. SALINGER
Served in the Army Signal Corps in World War II and also did counterintelligence work.

GUY DE MAUPASSANT
Was an army private during the Franco-Prussian War in 1870.

DICK FRANCIS
Served in the RAF during World War II.

NORMAN MAILER
Served with the armed forces in the Pacific during World War II. These experiences formed the kernel of *The Naked and the Dead*, the book that gave him his name and fame.

WILLIAM FAULKNER
Tried to enlist in the army during World War I but was rejected because of his diminutive stature (5' 5"). He joined the Royal Flying Corps in Canada afterward, but failed to see action.

JOHN DOS PASSOS
Was a member of the French Ambulance Service in World War I alongside e.e. cummings, Ernest Hemingway, and Walt Disney.

JOSEPH HELLER
Served in the U.S. Air Force during World War II.

ANTHONY BURGESS
Served with the Royal Army Medical Corps in World War II.

HERMAN WOUK
Served with the U.S. Naval Reserve destroying minesweepers from 1942 to 1946.

ALAN SILLITOE
Wireless operator with the RAF in Malaya from 1946 to 1949.

ARTHUR CONAN DOYLE
Army physician during the Boer War.

EDGAR WALLACE
Did army service in South Africa during the Boer War.

ARTHUR HAILEY
Served in the RAF during World War II.

DASHIELL HAMMETT
Was in the US Army during both world wars.

GORE VIDAL
Born at West Point military academy, he joined the U.S. Army Reserve Corps in 1943 rather than go to Harvard. His wartime experiences became the subject of his first two novels, *Williwaw* and *In a Yellow Wood*.

WALT WHITMAN
Was an army nurse for the Union forces during the American Civil War.

SAMUEL BECKETT
Fought in the French Resistance during World War II.

JAMES DICKEY
Joined the Air Force after his freshman year at university in 1941 and flew more than 100 combat missions altogether. "I look on existence from the point of view of a survivor," he said afterward. (He attributed his initial interest in writing to the long waits he had to endure between missions.)

MARQUIS DE SADE
Fought in the Seven Years War in 1829 when commissioned in the Royal Foot Guards.

GEORGE ORWELL
Fought in the Spanish Civil War with the POUM, a workers' party devoted to Marxism. He was wounded in the throat in the course of that war, an experience that he chronicled in his book *Homage to Catalonia* in 1937.

JUST FOLLOWING ORDERS
10 writers who were ministers of the cloth

JOHN DONNE
Ordained a priest in 1615 and became a Dean of St. Paul's
Cathedral five years later.

LAURENCE STERNE
Ordained in 1738, he was a parson for forty years.

JONATHAN SWIFT
Took Holy Orders in 1694 and became Dean of St. Patrick's
Cathedral in Dublin in 1713. The failure to secure a bishopric
wounded him deeply for the rest of his life while he malingered,
as he put it, "like a poisoned rat in a hole."

GERARD MANLEY HOPKINS
Was a Jesuit priest.

HORATIO ALGER
Became a Unitarian minister in 1864 but quit the pulpit twenty-
four years later. Rumor has it that he was sexually interfering
with the choirboys.

THOMAS MERTON
Was a Trappist monk. His immediate motivation was to atone for
what he termed his "pagan" past, but he also loved the isolation,
the rituals, the labor, and the vow of obedience.

RALPH WALDO EMERSON
Was ordained as a member of Boston's second church in 1829,
with a salary of $1,200 per annum.

JOHN BUNYAN
The son of a Bedfordshire tinker, he became a Nonconformist
preacher.

LEWIS CARROLL
The eldest son of a Cheshire rector, he was ordained himself in 1861.

GEORGE HERBERT
Metaphysical poet, clergyman, and also a keen musician.

LOST SOULS
5 authors who went missing or got lost

ANTOINE DE SAINT-EXUPÉRY
This author-cum-aviator took off on a reconnaissance mission over southern France in 1944 and was never seen again.

AMBROSE BIERCE
Traveled to revolutionary Mexico in 1913 and is believed to have died there a year later. His body was never found.

G. K. CHESTERTON
Was so forgetful that, he once got off a train and sent a telegram to his wife with the words, "Am in Market Harborough. Where ought I be?"

AGATHA CHRISTIE
In December 1926, she disappeared mysteriously after she found out that her husband was having an affair. Ten days later she was discovered in a health resort in Yorkshire, with rumors flying around that she had attempted suicide in the interim. (She later claimed that she'd had an attack of amnesia, brought on by the stress of her husband's infidelity and also the recent death of her mother.)

STEPHEN CRANE
Was missing at sea for several days after his ship sank while covering the war in Cuba. He was finally discovered adrift in a lifeboat and later recounted the story in *The Open Boat*.

WRITES OF WAY
25 authors' modus operandi

TRUMAN CAPOTE
Kept as many as 500 pencils sharpened before he attacked the page. He wrote his first draft on yellow paper; his second, on white; and the third and final one, on yellow again.

TENNESSEE WILLIAMS
Spoke his words aloud as he wrote.

HENRIK IBSEN
Started at 4 A.M. every day.

ANTHONY TROLLOPE
Malcolm Cowley said that Trollope was so persnickety about his routine of turning out exactly seven pages of text per day (and 49 per week) that, if he finished a novel halfway through the next day, he'd write the title of a new book on the next page and continue until he had completed the seven-page quota. He rose at 5.30 A.M. and often had his day's writing completed before breakfast.

GEORGES SIMENON
Like Trollope, he had an almost military regimen. His books all contained 200 pages and they were all written in eleven days, at a chapter a day. If this pattern were interrupted for any reason, he would simply abandon the book and start on another one instead.

ISAAC ASIMOV
Often worked as much as eighteen hours per day, producing more than fifty pages of text. (He typed at a speed of ninety words per minute.) His concentration was such, he said, that you could conduct an orgy in his office and he wouldn't look up.

ALEXANDRE DUMAS
Claimed that he only began writing his books when they were already completed in his head.

ANTHONY BURGESS
Wrote a great deal of *A Clockwork Orange* while drunk. This was to avoid being as shocked as he might have been otherwise by the coruscating nature of the material he was dealing with.

E. M. FORSTER
Liked to allow writing to happen rather than approach it with a preordained blueprint. As he put it himself, "How do I know what I think unless I see what I say?"

JOAN DIDION
Slept in the same room as her books in order to get closer to them and to enable her to write them better.

ERNEST HEMINGWAY
Always stopped writing when he was, as he put it, "going well," so that he wouldn't face the prospect of an empty page when he restarted.

HENRY DAVID THOREAU
Often wrote in the dark on a piece of paper he kept under his pillow whenever he was suffering from insomnia.

NOEL COWARD
Said he started every day by checking the obituary column in *The Times* to make sure that he was still alive, and then got down to work.

JANE AUSTEN
Was so private about her work that she usually wrote on tiny pieces of paper that could be hidden under blotters if anybody walked into the room during the heat of her inspiration.

G. K. CHESTERTON
Wrote everywhere the fancy took him: in cafés, bars, taxis, buses, and even against the walls of buildings in busy streets.

ERIC LINKLATER
Always said that he liked working unpredictable hours, adding: "Authors and uncaptured criminals are the only people in the world entirely free from routine."

GEORGE SAND
Wrote all her novels at night.

ROBERT FROST
Once, when the muse struck suddenly, he even took to writing on the sole of his shoe.

EDGAR ALLAN POE
Never sat down to write until he had completely arranged his plot and characters—and even their manner of speaking. To facilitate this, he paced the floor like an expectant father, getting himself psyched up for his big moment.

KATHERINE ANNE PORTER
Always wrote her last lines first, claiming that if she didn't know how a story ended she wouldn't know how to begin it.

SAMUEL PEPYS
Wrote in a private type of shorthand that wasn't deciphered until 1825—more than a century after his death.

THOMAS WOLFE

Is rumored to have mainly written in a standing position, using the top of his refridgerator as a desk.

JACK LONDON

Was so strapped during his early writing years—when the rejection slips were pouring in from editors—that he wrote on a battered old typewriter that would only print capital letters.

GRAHAM GREENE

Always said that he started work with the unconscious part of his mind in the mornings. In his second draft, the conscious mind took over in the afternoons. He reedited these pages before bedtime so that the subconscious part of his mind could evaluate them anew while he slept. Then, the following morning, he would be ready for the final draft.

ALEXANDER SOLZHENITSYN

When he was imprisoned in the gulag, he didn't dare to commit any of his ideas to paper for fear of confiscation (or worse), so he took to composing poetry in his head—because it was easier to remember than prose.

LOOT!

10 writers on money

"Being a novelist these days has almost nothing going for it. In terms of money and social status you would probably be far better off as a tea plantation worker in Sri Lanka."

Tom Davies

"Write out of love. Write out of instinct. Write out of reason. But always for money."

Louis Untermeyer

"The dubious privilege of a freelance writer is that he's given the freedom to starve wherever he likes."

S. J. Perelman

"Years ago, to say you were a writer was not the highest recommendation to your landlord. Today, he at least hesitates before he refuses to rent you an apartment. For all he knows, you may be rich."

Arthur Miller

"I never write 'metropolis' for seven cents because I can get the same price for 'city.' I never write 'policeman' because I can get the same money for 'cop'."

Mark Twain

"If you want to get rich from writing, write the sort of thing that's read by people who move their lips when they're reading to themselves."

Don Marquis

"Writing is finally play, and there's no reason why you should get paid for playing. If you're a real writer, you'll write no matter what."

Irwin Shaw

"I'm paid more than I deserve, but I'm not going to give any of it away. It's what kept Dickens going full tilt."

Tom Wolfe

"Money is exactly like sex. You think of nothing else if you don't have it, but other things if you do."

James Baldwin

"Annual income £20, annual expenditure nineteen ninety-six, result happiness. Annual income £20, annual expenditure twenty pounds eight and six, result misery."

Charles Dickens

GONE FOR BROKE
10 writers who died penniless

FRANCIS BACON
Was found guilty on twenty-three counts of corruption in 1621, and fined £40,000 — a blow from which he never recovered.

DASHIELL HAMMETT
Made a lot of money from his books and Hollywood screenplays, but also knew how to spend it. Neither were matters helped by the fact that his royalties were frozen during the McCarthy witch hunts.

GEORGE FARQUHAR
In 1703, this Irish playwright married a woman whom he believed was an heiress. He got a rude awakening when he learned that her finances were in an even worse state than his own, which was quite a feat.

OLIVER GOLDSMITH

Preferred the high life to knuckling down to work. He once saved the fare to go to America, but blew it before he got to the boat. On another occasion, he was bailed out of financial difficulties by his friend Samuel Johnson, who sold *The Vicar of Wakefield* to a publisher and got him £60 for it. Such benison never lasted long for this profligate, however: he died with debts of £2,000.

OSCAR WILDE

Imprisonment destroyed both his reputation and his bank balance. On his deathbed he's alleged to have said, "I'll die as I have lived—beyond my means."

HONORÉ DE BALZAC

Most of his business ventures failed: from mining to shipping to printing. He liked to shoot first and ask questions later, and he paid for such tempestuousness … with interest. He spent so much time avoiding creditors that he even built a secret entrance to his house for this express purpose.

DION BOUCICAULT

Died in poverty in New York after his plays went out of fashion. Was reduced to giving acting lessons to earn a living at the end of his life.

BRENDAN BEHAN

Behan drank his book advances, and any other money that was lying around. He also had a soft spot for unfortunates.

R. B. SHERIDAN

The destruction of his beloved Drury Lane Theatre by fire in 1809, coupled with an uncontrollable drinking habit and the loss of his Westminster seat three years later, meant that he was always struggling financially.

CORNELL WOOLRICH

Hard-boiled chronicler of grim fates, his output failed after his mother's death. He began living out of a suitcase in hotel rooms and had his leg amputated as a complication of his alcoholism. Died in obscurity in 1968.

MOMMIE DEAREST

10 writers who had mother fixations

ANDRÉ GIDE

His father died when he was only eleven and his mother believed he was too delicate for school, so she kept him at home. Here, she controlled every aspect of his life, from what he wore to what he read, and he was still under her thumb at the age of 25, when she died. He never shook off her influence.

W. SOMERSET MAUGHAM

Never quite recovered from the death of his mother from tuberculosis when he was 8.

J. M. BARRIE

His plucky mother, who had come through a difficult orphaned childhood, was a role model for him and he wrote a memoir of her (*Margaret Ogilvy*), as well as basing the character of Wendy in *Peter Pan* on her.

D. H. LAWRENCE

The victim not so much of mother love as smother love. His mother's arrant prudishness—which in part transmitted itself to him, albeit in an inverse fashion—gave him an ambition to crack Victorian England open through his writings. He had a love-hate relationship with her and she became a symbol of the life-denying philosophy he railed against. "I loved her like a lover," he confessed after her death. In many ways he was a closet prude, strongly disapproving of off-color stories and being anything but a proponent of casual sex. He always had to make it into a kind of spiritual sacrament. He once said, "Nothing nauseates me more than promiscuous sex."

GUSTAVE FLAUBERT
Was so enamored of his mother that he felt that no other woman could live up to her.

ERNEST HEMINGWAY
Referred to his mother as "The All-American Bitch" throughout his life, but could never shake off her influence on him. The great American macho man wasn't a mother's boy, but his rebellion against all things domestic was in part an overreaction against her thunderous influence on him in much the same way as Lawrence's was. When she died, he expressed a fear that she would rise out of her coffin for one last taunt at him. Much of his hatred came from the fact that she dressed him as a little girl in his youth.

MARCEL PROUST
Unnaturally devoted to his mother from childhood, he allowed himself be mollycoddled by her until her death in 1905. He carried the memory of her with him all his life.

STENDHAL
His mother died when he was 7 and he never quite recovered from the shock. He had semierotic thoughts about her all his life.

NORMAN MAILER
This serial groom insists that there's only one true Mrs. Mailer: his mom.

NATHANIEL HAWTHORNE
Developed a fixation with his mother after she became widowed when he was 4. He leaned on her for emotional solace, and vice versa.

MOMMY'S BOYS
5 authors raised without fathers

James Ellroy
Albert Camus
Raymond Chandler
Jack Kerouac
Jack London

N

MIDDLING TALENTS

25 writers who used their middle name as a first name

(William) Somerset Maugham
(Giles) Lytton Strachey
(Henry) Graham Greene
(Samuel) Dashiell Hammett
(Henry) Charles Bukowski
(Harry) Sinclair Lewis
(Mary) Flannery O'Connor
(Paul) Thomas Mann
(Pearl) Zane Grey
(Harold) Hart Crane
(Marvin) Neil Simon
(Joseph) Hilaire Belloc
(Frederick) Louis MacNeice
(Francis) Osbert Sitwell
(Adeline)Virginia Woolf
(Johann) August Strindberg
(Percy) Wyndham Lewis
(Nicole) Harper Lee
(Helen) Beatrix Potter
(Philip) Theodore Roethke
(Henry) Havelock Ellis
(Joseph) Rudyard Kipling
(Clarence) Malcolm Lowry
(Frederick) Ogden Nash
(Alfred) Damon Runyon

IN THE NAVY

5 writers who went to sea

TOBIAS SMOLLETT
A surgeon in the Royal Navy, started service aboard HMS *Chichester* in 1740.

HERMAN MELVILLE
Sailed for many years in the South Seas.

JACK LONDON
Became an oyster pirate in San Francisco Bay at the age of 15 and, soon after, became a deep-sea sailor.

JOSEPH CONRAD
Assumed his first command in Bangkok in 1888 after the captain of the *Otago* died at sea.

MALCOLM LOWRY
Went to sea on leaving school and based his novel, *Ultramarine*, on his experiences.

DESCENTS INTO HELL

10 writers who had nervous breakdowns

SIGMUND FREUD
Had a breakdown in the late 1890s after the lingering death of his father.

HORATIO ALGER
Revolted against his Puritan parents by going to Paris to live a bohemian life in 1852; suffered a breakdown on his return 12 years later.

HERMAN MELVILLE
Had a breakdown in 1855 due to frustration over the fact that he wasn't getting anywhere with his writing. Fame really only came posthumously.

RUPERT BROOKE
Suffered a breakdown a year after the death of his father in 1910.

VIRGINIA WOOLF
Had four major breakdowns during her life, most of them coinciding with the completion of novels. The last one pushed her over the edge and drove her to suicide.

EUGENE O'NEILL
Suffered a breakdown in 1912. The enforced rest led him to turn to writing as a career.

RUDYARD KIPLING
Born in India, Kipling grew up in England. He returned to India in 1881 at the age of 16 and began writing there. Fame befell him too suddenly, though, and he had a breakdown when he returned to London in 1889. (Nervous collapse features in his first published novel, *The Light That Failed*.)

CHARLES LAMB
Went to pieces following the collapse of his relationship with Ann Simmonds.

ALFRED LORD TENNYSON
His breakdown occurred after the death of his closest friend, Arthur Hallam, in 1883. (*In Memoriam* was written for him.)

TENNESSEE WILLIAMS
Had a breakdown in 1935, when his father, who disapproved of his writing ambitions, withdrew his financial support and sent him to business school instead. He took a night job in a shoe warehouse, but the strain of it all proved too much for him.

LAUREATES

20 English-language Nobel prize-winners

Rudyard Kipling (1907)

W. B. Yeats (1923)

George Bernard Shaw (1925)

Sinclair Lewis (1930)

John Galsworthy (1932)

Eugene O'Neill (1936)

Pearl S. Buck (1938)

T. S. Eliot (1948)

William Faulkner (1949)

Bertrand Russell (1950)

Sir Winston Churchill (1953)

Ernest Hemingway (1954)

John Steinbeck (1962)

Samuel Beckett (1969)

Patrick White (1973)

Saul Bellow (1976)

William Golding (1983)

Nadine Gordimer (1991)

Derek Walcott (1992)

Toni Morrison (1993)

OBSCURITIES

10 Nobel laureates it's unlikely you've read

Christian Matthais Theodor Mommsen (1902)
Bjornstjerne Martinus Bjornson (1903)
Jose Echegaray y Eizagirre (1904)
Selma Ottilia Lovisa Lagerlof (1909)
Erik Axel Karlfeldt (1931)
Frans Eemil Sillanpaa (1939)
Par Fabian Lagerkvist (1951)
Yasunari Kawabata (1968)
Karl Adolph Gjellerup (1971)
Odysseus Elytis (1979)

FAMOUS NOMINEES

15 writers who were nominated for the Nobel prize
but didn't win

Thomas Hardy
Joseph Conrad
Mark Twain
Henry James
Bertolt Brecht
Sean O'Casey
Marcel Proust
Virginia Woolf

F. Scott Fitzgerald
H. G. Wells
W. Somerset Maugham
Leo Tolstoy
Anton Chekhov
Henrik Ibsen
Graham Greene

DON'T GIVE UP THE DAY JOB
25 writers' occupations before they became famous

Truman Capote (Office boy at the *New Yorker*)
William S. Burroughs (Exterminator, private detective)
Sinclair Lewis (Janitor)
Malcolm Lowry (Longshoreman on steamer)
P. G. Wodehouse (Bank clerk)
Alan Sillitoe (Factory worker)
Tom Sharpe (Photographer)
Elmore Leonard (Advertising copywriter)
Patrick Kavanagh (Cobbler)
Sean O'Casey (Laborer)
Dick Francis (Jockey)
Mark Twain (Printer)
James Dickey (Advertising copywriter)
William Faulkner (Banker)
Yukio Mishima (Airport factory worker)
Sherwood Anderson (Manager of paint factory)
Fyodor Dostoevski (Military engineer)
John Arden (Architect)
Walt Whitman (Printer)
Sean O'Casey (Railway laborer)
Anne Sexton (Fashion model)
Fay Weldon (Advertising copywriter)
Raymond Chandler (Oil company executive)
T. S. Eliot (Bank official)
H. G. Wells (Dry goods store assistant)

SERVING TWO MASTERS

10 occupations concurrent with writing

Anthony Burgess (Composer)
Edward Lear (Landscape painter)
Roddy Doyle (Teacher)
Bram Stoker (Theater manager)
R. B. Sheridan (Politician)
Wallace Stevens (Lawyer)
John B. Keane (Innkeeper)
Robert Frost (Farmer)
Ted Hughes (Farmer)
Franz Kafka (Insurance clerk)

A GOOD START IS HALF THE WORK

10 classic book openings

"Ours is essentially a tragic age, so we refuse to take it seriously."

Lady Chatterley's Lover

"Mother died today."

The Outsider

"Miss Brooke had that kind of beauty which seems to be thrown into relief by poor dress."

Middlemarch

"It was love at first sight; the first time Yossarian saw the chaplain he fell madly in love with him."

Catch-22

191

"The past is a foreign country: they do things differently there."

The Go-Between

"It is a truth universally acknowledged, that a single man in possession of a good fortune must be in want of a wife."

Pride and Prejudice

"It was the best of times, it was the worst of times."

A Tale of Two Cities

"Happy families are all alike; every unhappy family is unhappy in its own way."

Anna Karenina

"Call me Ishmael."

Moby Dick

"It was a bright cold day in April and the clocks were striking thirteen."

1984

P

ANIMAL MAGNETISM

10 writers' pets

GERARD DE NERVAL
This nineteenth-century French poet kept a lobster as a pet, walking it each evening on a piece of ribbon he used as a leash.

CHARLES BAUDELAIRE
Kept a bat in a cage on his writing desk.

ALFRED LORD TENNYSON
Had a pony to pull around his wheelchair-bound wife.

HENRIK IBSEN
Kept a pet scorpion on his desk.

ROBERT BURNS
Liked his pet ewe so much that he wrote poems about her.

LORD BYRON
As well as a pet bear, he had ten horses, six dogs, three monkeys, five cats, an eagle, a parrot, a crow, a falcon, and five peacocks.

JOSEPH CONRAD
Kept a pet monkey with him during his seafaring days.

ANTON CHEKHOV
Had a crane that followed him everywhere he went.

ROBERT LOUIS STEVENSON
Kept a pet donkey, which features in his book *Travels with a Donkey*.

DANTE GABRIEL ROSSETTI
Kept a veritable zoo in his home, comprising cats, dogs, a monkey, zebra, raven, wombat, peacock, opossum, raccoon, woodchuck, and armadillo. He expressed an interest in buying an elephant to help him wash his windows by squirting the water through his trunk.

ADVENTURES IN THE SKIN TRADE
15 famous philanderers

GIACOMO CASANOVA
Claimed that he seduced 10,000 women, using pig's bladders as condoms. Chronicled in his autobiography are 132 of his female conquests, ninety-nine of which are of different nationalities, the youngest of which was 11, and the oldest, 52. One marathon session lasted seven hours and he once had sex with a woman twelve times in one day. He suffered from impotence toward the end of his life.

GUY DE MAUPASSANT
Professed to have bedded over a thousand woman and also said that he was capable of multiple orgasms and could "go" all night. Apparently, he was also talented at catering for women's needs.

JAMES BOSWELL
Often felt the urge for sex in the middle of a drinking session with his friends, whereupon he would leave them in order to seek relief with the nearest prostitute, then would return to his drink.

SAMUEL PEPYS
Suffered from—or maybe enjoyed—a condition called satyriasis (an insatiable appetite for sex). A small example will suffice: his wife caught him groping the maid one day and sacked her, but Pepys tracked her down to her new abode and continued his shenanigans.

KINGSLEY AMIS

Was frequently unfaithful to his wife Hillery. He was lying on a beach in Yugoslavia one day after an indiscretion she had exposed, and, in a fit of rage, she wrote "I Fuck Anything" on his back in lipstick. Years later, Amis authorized a photograph of himself with this message on his back to be used in his biography.

LORD BYRON

Enjoyed an action-packed sex life with innumerable mistresses and prostitutes, though most notably with Lady Caroline Lamb. When he jilted her she burned his effigy.

HONORÉ DE BALZAC

His mistresses ran into two figures. He married the last one, Louise Breugnol, seventeen years after they first met, but died five months later, at the age of 51.

GEORGES SIMENON

Claimed to have bedded more than a thousand women in his life, including a number of prostitutes.

MARQUIS DE SADE

His life was one long orgy of sadomasochistic frenzy, punctuated by gratuitous delight in inflicting pain on the unsuspecting. Had sex with anything that would stand still long enough.

WILKIE COLLINS

Was so sexually active that, at one point in his life, two of his mistresses, Caroline Graves and Martha Rudd, lived with him in his house at the same time.

OSCAR WILDE

Once boasted of bedding five boys at the same time—their lack of personal hygiene acted as an aphrodisiac.

NINON DE LENCLOS

Made love to 500 men, 439 of whom were monks.

VICTOR HUGO
Had sex with his wife Adele Foucher nine times on their wedding night. Was such a patron of brothels that, after he died, the French Government gave the prostitutes a grant to attend his funeral. They did this, wearing black scarves as a gesture of respect … around their privates.

ROBERT LOUIS STEVENSON
Was so highly sexed that he managed to keep the vast majority of Edinburgh's prostitutes in business, but also had a simultaneous urge to convert others to chastity. In the latter ambition, he even went so far as to read chapters from the Bible aloud to sheep in order to try and render them monastic.

ROBERT BURNS
A real lady's man, his life was mainly composed of casual infidelities and paternity suits.

FEAR AND LOATHING
5 writers' phobias

JAMES JOYCE
Was terrified of thunder, dogs, and firearms. During thunderstorms he used to hide in cupboards even in his adult years.

SIGMUND FREUD
Suffered from agoraphobia, and siderodromophobia, the fear of trains.

CHARLES DICKENS
Had a lifelong fear of bats.

THOMAS PEACOCK
Suffered all his life from a fear of fires. This proved to be prescient, as his house caught fire shortly before he died.

FYODOR DOSTOEVSKI
Had a terror of being buried alive. So great was the fear that, whenever he was sleeping away from home, he left a note at his bedside specifying that he wasn't to be buried immediately if it appeared to the person trying to wake him that he was dead.

ODD BODS
15 physical afflictions

CHARLES DICKENS
Had a lame left foot.

VOLTAIRE
Suffered from chronic constipation all his life, and was so desperate to find a cure that he once swallowed lead shot on a quack doctor's instructions.

SAMUEL PEPYS
Was accidentally made sterile by an operation to remove his gallstones.

ALDOUS HUXLEY
A childhood illness left him partially blind, which meant that he had to learn Braille.

LORD BYRON
His foot was so crippled that he once begged a doctor to amputate it.

WILLIAM WORDSWORTH
Had no sense of smell, despite the fact that he liked writing about flowers so much.

F. SCOTT FITZGERALD
His wife Zelda told him that his penis was too small for him to be sexually attractive to her, which sent him into a decline.

JULES VERNE
Wounded in the foot when his insane nephew shot him, which resulted in a lifelong limp.

CHRISTOPHER NOLAN
Deprivation of oxygen at his birth left him with severe brain damage, but his mother realized that he had a sharp mind and taught him the alphabet. He started to write by placing a unicorn stick on his forehead, and went on to become a famous poet and playwright.

ANNA SEWELL
The author of *Black Beauty* was an invalid for most of her life.

JOSEPH HELLER
Suffers from the Guillain-Barré syndrome (a viral condition, not unlike polio, that attacks the nervous system). As he puts it: "Any disease named after two people has to be crap." In 1986, he wrote about it in tragicomic fashion in *No Laughing Matter*.

ARNOLD BENNETT
Had to wear cast-iron braces as a child because of a bent leg.

ELIZABETH BARRETT BROWNING
Bedridden for most of her life as a result of a spinal injury she suffered at the age of 15.

ANTONIN ARTAUD
Had an unusually large nose, which resulted in him fighting many duels whenever people made fun of it.

EUGENE O'NEILL
Wrote little or nothing for the last two years of his life because of a nervous disease that caused his hands to shake involuntarily.

THE SINCEREST FORM OF FLATTERY
10 writers on plagiarism

"If a writer has to rob his mother, he will not hesitate. The 'Ode to a Grecian Urn' is worth any number of old ladies."

William Faulkner

"I thought Hemingway's prose was perfect until I read Stephen Crane and realized where he got it from."

Gore Vidal

"Everything I've ever said will be credited to Dorothy Parker."

George S. Kaufman

"Immature poets imitate; mature poets steal."

T. S. Eliot

"Cynics have claimed that there are only six basic plots. *Frankenstein* and *My Fair Lady* are really the same story."

Leslie Halliwell

"The eighth commandment wasn't made for bards."

Samuel Taylor Coleridge

"If we steal thoughts from the moderns, it will be cried down as plagiarism; if from the ancients, it will be cried down as erudition."

Charles Caleb Colton

"Adam was the only man who, when he said a good thing, knew that nobody had said it before him."

Mark Twain

"I borrow from others shamelessly, but only from the best."

Thornton Wilder

"Nothing is new except arrangement."

Will Durant

YOU CAN QUOTE ME ON THAT
10 poetic lines that have passed into common usage

"Stone walls do not a prison make
Nor iron bars a cage"

Alexander Pope, 'The Dunciad'

"The best laid schemes o' mice and men/Gang aft-a-gley."

Robert Burns, 'To a Mouse'

"A thing of beauty is a joy forever."

John Keats, 'Ode to a Grecian Urn'

"No man is an island."

John Donne, 'Devotions'

"All hope abandon, ye who enter here."

John Milton, *Paradise Lost*

"East is East and West is West and never the twain shall meet."

Rudyard Kipling, 'The Ballad of East and West'

"All hell broke loose."

John Milton, *Paradise Lost*

"To err is human, to forgive divine."

Alexander Pope, *An Essay on Confession*

"The female of the species is more deadly than the male."

Rudyard Kipling, 'The Female of the Species'

"Heaven has no rage like a love to hate turned/Nor hell a fury, like a woman scorned."

William Congreve, 'The Mourning Bride'

FROM BAD TO VERSE
10 poets on poetry

"I believe technique is important. If most people who called themselves poets were tightrope-walkers, they'd be dead."

Michael Longley

"With a lyric poem you look, meditate and put the rock back. With fiction you poke things with a stick to see what will happen."

Margaret Atwood

"In youth, poems come to you out of the blue. They're delivered at your doorstep like the morning news. But when you get older you have to dig."

Stanley Kunitz

"I keep Friday as my poetry writing day, and I have to arrange for the muse to attend between 10 A.M. and 4 P.M."

Alison Chisholm

"Poetry is like solving a crossword puzzle in which you are also the compiler."

Don Paterson

"The only people who have trouble with poetry are the people who link it with literature. It's much more akin to mountain-walking, and dancing by yourself at 2 A.M."

Theo Dorgan

"Poets, like whores, are only hated by each other."

William Wycherley

"A poetry best-seller is any book that sells four or five copies in a given store."

Michael Wiegers

"Parents still prefer their children to be taxidermists and tax collectors rather than poets."

Charles Simic

"A poem is never finished, merely abandoned."

Paul Valery

BETWEEN TWO STOOLS

5 politicians who wrote novels

BENITO MUSSOLINI

Wrote *The Cardinal's Mistress* in 1909 when he was working as a labor union official. It came about as the result of a request from the editor to fill the weekly fiction slot of the socialist newspaper to which he contributed.

WINSTON CHURCHILL

Wrote *Savrola* in 1898 when he was 23 years of age and serving as an army officer in India. The plot, perhaps inevitably, is political in nature.

JEFFREY ARCHER

Former deputy chairman of the Conservative Party under Margaret Thatcher. Since the publication of *Not a Penny More, Not a Penny Less* in 1975, the novelistic output of the sometime politician has grown almost as much as his bank balance.

BENJAMIN DISRAELI

Born in a library, Disraeli wrote *Coningsby* in 1844 and *Sybil* four years later. He once exclaimed, "When I want to read a novel, I write one."

ANDRÉ MALRAUX

Author of *The Human Condition* and other novels, he held various ministerial posts in de Gaulle's government over a twenty-year period.

BOOK YOUR SEAT
15 writers who ran for political office

VICTOR HUGO
Candidate for the French presidency in 1848.

JACK LONDON
Socialist candidate for the mayoralty of his home town in
California in 1905.

H. G. WELLS
Stood as Labour candidate for English Parliament in 1921 and 1922.

UPTON SINCLAIR
Twice a socialist nominee for the position of Governor of
California, once a candidate for the U.S. Senate, and, in 1934, won
the primary gubernatorial nomination for the Democratic Party.

GORE VIDAL
Won the Democratic nomination for Congress in New York in
1960.

JAMES MICHENER
Democratic candidate for Congress in Pennsylvania in 1962.

NORMAN MAILER
Ran for Mayor of New York in a high-profile 1969 campaign
with the slogan "No More Bullshit." Unfortunately, most people
felt that what he was peddling was just a different kind of bullshit and he came fourth out of five contenders.

HUNTER S. THOMPSON
The maverick scribe was more surprised than anybody else to
receive electoral support when he ran for Sheriff of Pitkin
County in Colorado in 1970.

CLARE BOOTHE LUCE
Elected to the House of Representatives as a Republican and also became U.S. Ambassador to Italy in 1952.

BENJAMIN DISRAELI
Was the first Conservative Prime Minister of Britain in 1868, and again in 1874, after a short hiatus.

ARCHIBALD MACLEISH
The American poet became U.S. Assistant Secretary of State in 1944, he also helped draft the constitution of UNESCO.

HUGH MACDIARMID
Founder of the Scottish Nationalist Party.

C. P. SNOW
Parliamentary Secretary to the Minister of Science and Technology.

W. B. YEATS
Elected senator of the Irish Free State in 1922 and served in that capacity for the next six years.

ANTHONY TROLLOPE
Described standing as a Liberal candidate for parliament in 1868 as "the most wretched fortnight of my manhood." He came last, with only 740 votes.

FEELING BLUE
10 authors who wrote pornography or erotica

GEORGES BATAILLE
The master of surrealist erotica that tests the boundaries of sexual taboo, with scenes both horrific and strangely sensuous.

D. H. LAWRENCE
Frequently castigated for being pornographic in many of his works, principally his last novel *Lady Chatterley's Lover*. But he always resolutely denied that he wished to titillate.

ANAÏS NIN
This renowned diarist and onetime lover of Henry Miller wrote the strongly erotic *Delta of Venus* when she was short of cash in the late 1960s.

MARK TWAIN
His most famous (or infamous) pornographic work is *1601*, which he wrote in 1880. "If there's a decent word findable in it," he said, "it is because I overlooked it."

MARQUIS DE SADE
Lived a life of scandalous sexual debauchery and wrote his pornographic chronicles of sexual perversion while he was in the Bastille and other prisons.

HENRY MILLER
Three of his early novels, *Tropic of Cancer*, *Black Spring*, and *Tropic of Capricorn*, were seized by U.S. Customs on publication because of their allegedly pornographic content.

ANNE RICE
Famous for her *Vampire Chronicles*, she wrote two erotic novels in the 1980s under the pseudonym Anne Rampling.

ALEXANDER TROCCHI
The Scottish beatnik wrote erotica for Maurice Girodias' Olympia Press under the pseudonym Frances Lengel.

LEOPOLD VON SACHER-MASOCH
The kinky author of *Venus in Furs* who gave birth to the term "masochism."

GUILLAUME APOLLINAIRE

The celebrated Futurist poet supplemented his income by writing erotica with titles such as *Flesh Unlimited* and *Eleven Thousand Virgins*.

DARK AS THE GRAVE WHEREIN MY FRIEND IS LAID

10 books published posthumously that have become classics

The Mystery of Edwin Drood Charles Dickens
Confederacy of Dunces John Kennedy Toole
Brief Lives John Aubrey
Everything That Rises Must Converge Flannery O'Connor
Remembrance of Things Past Marcel Proust
A Moveable Feast Ernest Hemingway
The Third Policeman Flann O'Brien
Long Day's Journey into Night Eugene O'Neill
The Last Tycoon F. Scott Fitzgerald
The Professor Charlotte Brontë

TRICK OR TREAT

5 literary pranksters

VOLTAIRE

When bored by guests, he used to pretend to faint in order to get rid of them.

GIACOMO CASANOVA
Once dug up a corpse and cut an arm off it. He hid it under a friend's bed and tugged at the sheets. When his friend reached under the bed to find out who was there, Casanova handed him the severed hand. The man got such a shock that he had a stroke and was paralyzed for life.

ALGERNON CHARLES SWINBURNE
Outraged the company in the house in Chelsea that he shared with the painter Rossetti—by sliding naked down the banisters.

PERCY BYSSHE SHELLEY
When he was at Eton in 1804, he gave his teacher an electric shock by wiring his doorknob to a machine that generated electricity.

BRENDAN BEHAN
Put sacks over the windows of a woman he disliked so that she'd think she was blind when she woke up the next morning.

ALTAR EGOS
5 writers who contemplated becoming preachers

THOMAS HARDY
Considered taking holy orders in the mid-1860s when he was an architect's apprentice, but he abandoned the idea when he developed agnostic tendencies.

CHARLES LAMB
A stutter prevented him from realizing his ambition.

GIACOMO CASANOVA

During his first sermon, a pretty girl distracted him. She got away, but on leaving the church that day he picked up a pair of sisters and deflowered them instead. End of vocation.

OLIVER GOLDSMITH

The son of a rector, he considered taking holy orders himself, but was rejected on the grounds of his unacademic nature and bohemian lifestyle.

THOMAS CARLYLE

In 1813 studied at Edinburgh University for the Presbyterian ministry, but didn't last the pace, finding the appeal of the lay world too great. He went on to become a math teacher and then a journalist.

POW WOW

10 writers who were prisoners of war

E.E. CUMMINGS

Imprisoned in 1917 while working for the Ambulance Corps in France as part of the war effort. His experiences there formed the nexus of his book *The Enormous Room*.

MIGUEL CERVANTES

Joined the Spanish Army and fought at the Battle of Lepanto. He and his brother were captured by the Turks in 1576 and imprisoned for five years in Algiers. He was ransomed in 1580.

JEAN-PAUL SARTRE

Served in the French Army as a weatherman during World War II and was captured and jailed by the Germans in 1940.

Six months later he, was released and joined the French Resistance as a propagandist.

KURT VONNEGUT
Joined the U.S. Infantry in World War II and was captured during the Battle of the Bulge. He witnessed the firebombing of Dresden as a P.O.W. (chronicling it in *Slaughterhouse 5*) and after the war he was decorated with the Purple Heart.

GEOFFREY CHAUCER
Fought in the army of Edward III in 1360. He was imprisoned by the French at the siege of Reims and Edward paid a ransom of £16 to have him freed.

EZRA POUND
Jailed in 1945 for broadcasting on Rome Radio material that was hostile to the U.S.A.'s wartime interests. In 1945, he was imprisoned in what was euphemistically called an American Disciplinary Training Center. The treatment he received there was near barbaric. He was kept in solitary confinement for months at a time. No doubt his subsequent mental illness was in part caused by these horrific conditions.

PRIMO LEVI
This Italian Jew formed an anti-Nazi guerrilla unit in World War II, but was betrayed in 1943 and turned over to the SS, who sent him to Auschwitz. He would probably have died there were it not for the fact that a bout of scarlet fever caused him to be evacuated: his captors feared its contagiousness.

CESARE PAVESE
Arrested by Fascists in 1935 for suspected membership of the Italian Resistance. He was confined to the village of Branceleone Calabro for ten months as a result.

HEINRICH BÖLL
Became a prisoner of war in 1945 after serving in the German Army during World War II.

ROBERT LOWELL
A prisoner of war in his own country. Imprisoned for being a conscientious objector in 1943.

WRITE ON!

25 prolific authors (number of works in brackets)

Lope de Vega (2,200)
Jose Carlos Inoue (1,046)
Kathleen Lindsey (904)
Enid Blyton (700)
Barbara Cartland (636)
John Creasey (565)
Ronald Ridout (515)
Ursula Bloom (500)
Georges Simenon (400)
Isaac Asimov (300)
Alexandre Dumas (272)
Lewis Carroll (255)
Daniel Defoe (250)
Edgar Wallace (173)
P. G. Wodehouse (120)
Hilaire Belloc (100)
George Sand (100)
Robert Graves (100)
Ezra Pound (90)

Honoré de Balzac (85)
Earle Stanley Gardner (80)
Upton Sinclair (80)
Agatha Christie (78)*
Colette (73)
Zane Grey (65)

* This figure represents her crime novels. She also wrote nineteen plays and six romantic novels under the pseudonym Mary Westmacott.

I DON'T

10 proposals of marriage that were rejected

JANE AUSTEN
She accepted the marriage proposal of 21-year-old Harris Bigg-Wither one evening, but by the following morning she had changed her mind. Such resolve was to stay with her and she died unmarried.

FRANZ KAFKA
Proposed to Felice Bauer in a letter in this hardly enthusiastic manner: "Marry me and you will regret it. Marry me not and you will regret it. Marry me or marry me not and you will regret either." It wasn't, you have to admit, a very good deal for her and she chose the slightly more attractive proposition of searching for marital happiness without him.

AGATHA CHRISTIE

Was once proposed to by a colonel fifteen years older than her. Her mother advised her to tell him to wait six months to see if he still felt the same way about her then. After the allotted time span, he sent her a telegram saying, "Can't stand this indecision any longer—will you marry me?" She said no.

LYTTON STRACHEY

Was involved in an unusual situation. He proposed to Virginia Woolf (an achievement in itself, considering he was gay), but withdrew his offer the following day—after she had accepted it. "I was in terror lest she would kiss me," he explained.

W. B. YEATS

Proposed to Maud Gonne MacBride, who became his life's obsession, on numerous occasions but she rejected him each time. The birth pangs of some of his most beautifully bittersweet lyrics lay in such rejection.

JOHN MILLINGTON SYNGE

Proposed twice to Cherrie Matheson when he was 24, but she refused him on religious grounds. She was a member of a strict religious sect—the Plymouth Brethren—which forbade marital congress with nonbelievers such as Synge.

OSCAR WILDE

Proposed to Charlotte Montefiore in 1881, but she refused. He wrote back to her saying, "I am so sorry about your decision. With your money and my brain we could have gone so far."

JONATHAN SWIFT

His friend Esther Vanhomrigh (whom he called Vanessa by combining the first parts of her first name and surname—albeit back to front) asked him to marry her. He rebuffed her proposal in the most public manner possible, in his poem 'Cademus and Vanessa.'

GEORGE BERNARD SHAW

Freethinking Annie Besant once proposed to him by handing him a private contract to replace the traditional religious and civil ones. However, it was so convoluted that it was worse than the contract it replaced, and he refused to sign it.

JOHN RUSKIN

Proposed marriage to 18-year-old art student Rose La Touche when he was 47, but was rejected after she heard of his impotence on his wedding night with former wife Euphemia Gray.

POLITICAL CENSURE

5 authors who were prosecuted by the State for their writings

THEODORE REINKING

This Danish author was put in jail in 1644 for writing a book that offended the Swedish nation. After some years of incarceration, he was informed that he was going to be executed if he didn't, literally, eat his words, so he swallowed a copy of his book page by page. His jailers magnanimously offered him some sauce to help him to digest it better.

DANIEL DEFOE

Was imprisoned in 1702 after he published a pamphlet in which he suggested that all nonconformist preachers (of whom he was one) should be hanged. His words were meant to be ironic, but they were taken almost literally by the ecclesiastical establishment of the day.

VOLTAIRE

Imprisoned in the Bastille for one year in 1717 for lampooning the Duc d'Orléans.

MARQUIS DE SADE
Served fifteen days behind bars in 1801 for lampooning
Napoleon in a pamphlet. (He had already had a death sentence
for a sex offense commuted in 1772.)

ALEXANDER SOLZHENITSYN
Was promoted to the rank of captain when fighting against the
Nazis at the Russian front in 1944. He was becoming disillusioned
with Stalin, however, and in the course of a letter home he made
a joke about (of all things) his mustache. The letter was intercepted
by the N.K.V.D. (the forerunners of the K.G.B.) and in February
of the following year he was sentenced to eight years' hard labor
for, as the N.K.V.D. put it, "disseminating anti-Soviet propaganda."
(If only Stalin had shaved!) There was no trial, and for the next
ten years he was either a prisoner in the gulag or in internal
exile.

MODEL BEHAVIOR
20 real-life prototypes for literary characters

GUSTAVE VON ASCHENBACH
Thomas Mann's hero from *Death in Venice* was based on the
composer Gustav Mahler.

UNCLE TOM
The prototype for Harriet Beecher Stowe's black slave was one
Josiah Henson, who achieved fame as a Methodist preacher after
escaping from the South.

STELLA
Jonathan Swift's figure of awe in his *Journal to Stella* was really
Esther Johnson, for whom he felt special affection all his life.

SHYLOCK

Shakespeare's penny-pinching debt collector was based on the Jewish doctor Roderigo Lopez, who was hanged for conspiring to kill one of his own patients in 1592.

BUCK MULLIGAN

This outrageously laddish character from *Ulysses* was based on Joyce's surgeon friend Oliver St. John Gogarty. Gogarty was an author in his own right but, to his eternal chagrin, garnered more publicity from the Mulligan portrait than from his own works.

MICAWBER

Dickens' father John was the inspiration behind this eternal optimist.

SHERLOCK HOLMES

Holmes had his origins in a surgeon friend of Arthur Conan Doyle's called Joseph Bell. He had uncanny powers of observation and diagnosis, which intrigued Conan Doyle.

GUDRUN BRANGWEN

Lawrence used Katherine Mansfield as the basis for Gudrun, who appears in both *The Rainbow* and *Women in Love*.

MONROE STAHR

F. Scott Fitzgerald based this character from *The Last Tycoon* on ill-fated movie *wunderkind* Irving Thalberg.

CAPTAIN AHAB

Based on Owen Chase, the first mate of a ship sunk by a sperm whale. He spent ninety-one days adrift on a small boat afterward, having to eat the corpse of one of his dead friends in order to avoid starving to death.

VON HUMBOLDT FLEISCHER

The poet drunk in Saul Bellow's *Humboldt's Gift* is modeled on the doomed bohemian poet Delmore Schwartz.

JAY GATSBY
F. Scott Fitzgerald modeled his most famous creation partly on himself, but mostly on a Long Island bootlegger called Max Gerlach.

HEDDA GABLER
Gabler came from a young lady with whom Ibsen was infatuated toward the end of his life. Her name was Emilie Bardach.

VICTOR FRANKENSTEIN
The poet Percy Bysshe Shelley partly inspired (if that's the correct word) this creation of his wife Mary, as did the alchemist Konrad Dippel.

DRACULA
Bram Stoker's Transylvanian vampire was based partly on a Turkish tyrant called Vlad the Impaler, whose reign of terror ran from 1456 to 1462, and partly on actor Henry Irving, whom he managed for many years.

HUMPHREY CHIMPDEN EARWICKER
Joyce modeled this elusive character from *Finnegan's Wake* on his father.

HUCKLEBERRY FINN
Huck came from a Tom Blankenship, the son of the local drunkard in Hannibal, Mark Twain's hometown.

CLIFFORD CHATTERLEY
Lady Chatterley's husband was based on the textile manufacturer William Arkwright, who was rendered impotent after a horse-riding accident in the late 1870s.

BROADBENT
H. G. Wells saw this character from George Bernard Shaw's *John Bull's Other Island* as a parody of himself, which did not please him very much.

ROBINSON CRUSOE

Daniel Defoe based Crusoe on the seafarer Alexander Selkirk, who objected to the conditions on a ship on which he was employed in 1704 and asked to be put ashore on a tiny desert island in the Pacific Ocean off South America. He lived alone there for four years and four months, and Defoe used his experiences as the basis for Crusoe.

ALL'S WELL THAT STARTS WELL

The sources of 5 proverbs

"Half a loaf is better than no bread."
Charles Kingsley's Alton Locke, 1850

"Fools and their money are easily parted."
Tobias Smollett's Roderick Random, 1661

"Spare the rod and spoil the child."
Thomas Fuller's Gnomologa, 1732

"It's hard to teach an old dog new tricks."
William Camden's Remains Concerning Britain, 1670

"The last straw breaks the camel's back."
Florence Nightingale's Notes on Nursing, 1861

SUE DE NYM

40 writers' pseudonyms (real names in brackets)

Jean Rhys (Gwen Williams)
Ivan Petrovich Belkin (Alexander Pushkin)
Guy de Valmont (Guy de Maupassant)
James Hadley Chase (Rene Raymond)
Saki (Hector Munro)
James Herriot (James Alfred Wright)
Voltaire (François-Marie Arouet)
Lewis Carroll (Charles Lutwidge Dodgson)
John Le Carré (David Cornwell)
George Orwell (Eric Blair)
Molière (Jean-Baptiste Poquelin)
Pablo Neruda (Ricardo Neftali Reyes)
Anatole France (Jacques Anatole François Thibault)
Alberto Moravia (Alberto Pincherle)
Stendhal (Marie Henri Beyle)
O. Henry (William Sydney Porter)
Maxim Gorki (Aleksei Peshkov)
Elia (Charles Lamb)
Lenny Bruce (Leonard Alfred Schneider)
Bob Dylan (Robert Zimmermann)
Hugh MacDiarmid (Christopher Murray Grieve)
Guillaume Apollinaire (Wilhelm Apollonaris de Kostrowitsky)
Compton Mackenzie (Edward Montague Compton)
Harold Robbins (Francis Kane)
Edgar Wallace (Richard Horatio)
Q. Moonblood (Sylvester Stallone)
Andrew Lee (Louis Auchincloss)
Colette (Sidonie Gabrielle)

George Sand (Amandine Dupin)
Isak Dinesen (Karen Blixen)
Fanny Burney (Madame d'Arblay)
Elizabeth Bowen (Elizabeth Dorothea Cole)
Martin Ross (Violet Martin)
Brinsley MacNamara (John Weldon)
Frank O'Connor (Michael O'Donovan)
A. E. (George Russell)
Seán O'Faoláin (John Francis Whelan)
The Man in the Cloak (James Clarence Mangan)
Patricius Walker (William Allingham)
George A. Bermingham (Canon James Owen Hannay)

IDENTITY CRISES
15 writers who have used both a pen name and their real name (real name in brackets)

Georges Sim (Georges Simenon)
Richard Bachman (Stephen King)
Peter Collinson (Dashiell Hammett)
William Lee (William S. Burroughs)
Nicholas Blake (Cecil Day-Lewis)
Roland Allen (Alan Ayckbourn)
Robert Markham (Kingsley Amis)
Frank Baker (Sir Richard Burton)
Charles Norden (Lawrence Durrell)
William Irish (Cornell Woodrich)
Barbara Vine (Ruth Rendell)
Rose Blight (Germaine Greer)

Jane Somers (Doris Lessing)
Corno di Basseto (George Bernard Shaw)
Michael Bryan (Brian Moore)

WHAT'S IN A NAME?
10 authors who had particular reasons for using pseudonyms

HUGH LEONARD
His real name is Jack Keyes Byrne, but in the early years of his literary career he submitted a play to the Abbey Theater with a character called Hugh Leonard in it. It was rejected, so the next time he submitted a play he called himself Hugh Leonard for mischief. It was accepted, so he kept the pseudonym and has used it ever since. Only his real friends call him Jack, he insists.

OSCAR WILDE
Wrote as Sebastian Melmoth after coming out of prison, the name "Oscar Wilde" having been besmirched by then. 'The Ballad of Reading Gaol' was published under the pseudonym "3.3," his prison number.

MARK TWAIN
His real name was Samuel Clemens. He took on "Mark Twain" because of his love for riverboating. It's a nautical term meaning "two fathoms deep." (Some of his early works were also published under the pseudonym Thomas Jefferson Snodgrass.)

YUKIO MISHIMA
His real name was Kimitake Hiraoka. He changed it so that his antiliterary father wouldn't know that he wrote. (Translated into English it means "mysterious devil bewitched with death.")

CHARLOTTE BRONTË
Adopted the pseudonym Currer Bell as she wrote in an age where it wasn't deemed fitting for a woman to put pen to paper. Likewise for her sisters Emily/Ellis Bell and Anne/Acton Bell. When the first series of books by the siblings appeared, the publishers used curiosity about the real identity of the authors as a publicity device, fueling speculation that one woman wrote them all. Charlotte and Anne weren't impressed by this ploy, and had to visit the publishers in person in 1848 to quell such rumors.

DALTON TRUMBO
Wrote under the names "Robert Rich" and "Howard Fast" after being blacklisted as one of the "Hollywood Ten" during the reds-under-the-beds purge of Joe McCarthy and Co.

REBECCA WEST
Her real name is Cicily Isabel Fairfield. She chose the pen name because of her admiration for the heroine of Ibsen's Rosmersholm.

ALBERT CAMUS
Wrote under the pseudonym of "Bauchard" when composing anti-Nazi tracts for *La Peste* newspaper during World War II in France. Was interrogated many times for involvement in the French Resistance, and he lived in constant fear of being deported to a concentration camp.

FORD MADOX FORD
His real name was Ford Madox Hueffer. He changed his surname during the anti-German hysteria that accompanied the outbreak of World War I.

BRIAN O'NOLAN

Flann O'Brien/Myles na Gopaleen was an Irish civil servant. During his time in office there was a stipulation in Ireland against this lowly breed having the audacity to write. He therefore used various pseudonyms when writing his novels, and his column, *Cruiskeen Lawn*, in the *Irish Times*.

THE NAME GAME

10 writers with multiple pseudonyms

Konstantin Arsenivich Mikhailov (325)*
Georges Simenon (23)
John Creasey (25)
Charles Hamilton (24)
Jonathan Swift (15)
William Makepeace Thackeray (11)
Brian O'Nolan (10)
Percy Bysshe Shelley (5)
Evan Hunter (5)
Sir Walter Scott (5)

* This is a Russian comedian who was born in 1868. Most of the pseudonyms are merely abbreviations.

10 PSEUDONYMS OF BRIAN O'NOLAN

Flann O'Brien
Myles na Gopaleen
Lir O'Connor
John J. Dowe
James Knowall
Jimmy Cunning
Count O'Blather
Stephen Blakesley
The Cruiskeen Lawn
Brian O'Nualláin

5 PSEUDONYMS OF EVAN HUNTER

Ed McBain
Ezra Hannon
Curt Cannon
Hunt Collins
Richard Marsten

5 PSEUDONYMS OF WALTER SCOTT

Captain Clutterbuck
Lawrence Templeton
Malachi Malagrowther
Crystal Croftangry
Jebediah Cleisbotham

15 PSEUDONYMS OF JONATHAN SWIFT

The Great Dean
A Shoeboy
Gregory miso-Sarum
Simon Wagstaff
Abel Ripper
Lemuel Gulliver
Dr. Andrew Tripe
Presto
T. Fribble
T. N. Philomath
Jack Frenchman
M. B. Drapier
M'Flor O'Squarr
Isaac Bickerstaff

10 PSEUDONYMS OF WILLIAM MAKEPEACE THACKERAY

Michael Angelo Titmarsh
Dorothea Julia Ramsbottom
Our Fat Contributor
Frederick Haltamount de Montmorency
Fitzjeames de la Pluche
Paul Pinder
Miss Tickletoby
George Savage Fitzboodle
C. J. Yellowplush
Theophile Wagstaff

5 PSEUDONYMS OF PERCY BYSSHE SHELLEY

Mr. Jones
Jeremiah Stukeley
Victor
The Hermit of Marlow
John Fitzvictor

A PENN'ORTH OF ALL SORTS
20 publishing curiosities

Japanese politician Uichi Noda wrote 1307 letters to his wife between 1961 and 1985. They were published in twenty-five volumes, which run to more than 12,000 pages.

Robber James Allen left orders that after he died his autobiography should be bound in his own skin and presented to one of his victims as a sign of his remorse. This was done in 1837.

Tobias Smollett organized a unique publicity drive for his *Complete History of England* in 1761 … by bribing sacristans to put fliers for it in church pews.

The first poem from Dylan Thomas ever printed ('His Requiem') wasn't his own, but was cadged from a comic called *The Boy's Own Paper*. It was only after it became famous and the poem was republished as a curiosity piece that the plagiarism was discovered.

Washington Irving—who used the pseudonym "Diedrich Knickerbocker"—went one better in 1809, drumming up publicity for his book *History of New York* by leaking a series of false news items about himself. One story said that he had mysteriously disappeared from his lodgings, but he left a manuscript behind. The landlord, the story went, had it published to recoup the rent outstanding. The public lapped it all up and the book went on to become a bestseller.

Mark Twain reviewed his own book *The Innocents Abroad* anonymously in 1869.

The largest ever British publication is the 1,112-volume *British Parliamentary Papers*, published by the Irish University Press. The full set weighs over three tons. It would take six years to finish if one were to spend ten hours a day reading it. Its production involved £15,000 worth of gold ingots and the skins of 34,000 Indian goats.

The smallest book ever printed was the 1985 reprint of the children's story *Old King Cole* by Gleniffer Press. Eighty-five copies of this were printed. It measures $1/25$th of an inch square and the pages can only be turned with a needle.

Georges Perec wrote a book called *La Disparition* (Avoid), which didn't use the letter "e." This was topped by the English translator Gilbert Adair, who managed to replicate that feat. (Perec also wrote a novel that contains no other vowels *except* "e.")

A bibliophile called Captain Maurice Hamonneau has bound a copy of Adolf Hitler's *Mein Kampf* in (appropriately enough) skunk skin. He also has a copy of *All Quiet on the Western Front* bound in a World War I uniform.

In 1953 there was a fireproof edition of Ray Bradbury's *Fahrenheit 451* published on asbestos boards.

B. S. Johnson's novel-in-a-box *The Unfortunates* (1969) came in twenty-seven loose-leaf sections, to be read in any order.

In 1996, a book called *What Men Know About Women* appeared, which consisted of 200 blank pages.

Another enterprising publisher put out a book called *How To Be Taller*. This also contained nothing more than blank pages, but the blurb had a piece of useful advice: "Stand on this book."

Richard Templeton, Jr. wrote a book called *The Quick Brown Fox,* which has thirty-three sentences in it—each containing all twenty-six letters of the alphabet (like the title of the book).

Jerzy Andrzejewski's *The Gates of Paradise* has no periods until the very last page of the book.

Timothy Dexter wrote a book in 1802 called *A Pickle for the Knowing Ones* that has no punctuation at all. In 1838, however, he added a page to the book with various grammatical appendages like colons, semicolons, commas, exclamation points, etc. He suggested that these were for readers to scatter through-out the text wherever they wished.

When the mistress of the novelist Eugene Sue died, she left her skin to him in her will, with instructions that he should bind a book with it. He obliged.

When Edgar Wallace's *The Four Just Men* was published, he offered readers £500 if they could guess correctly how the murder was committed. Correct answers poured in with such frequency that Wallace excluded himself from his royalties.

John Creasey claimed to have received no fewer than 743 rejection slips from publishers before his first book was accepted in 1932. It is said that he typed the whole text on the back of the 743 letters. Revenge is sweet.

A great practical joker, Scottish novelist Alasdair Gray once had his publishers put an erratum slip in the first edition of a novel of his which read: "this erratum slip has been inserted by mistake."

R

READ ALL ABOUT IT
10 writers on readers and reading

"I think we ought to read only the kind of books that wound and stab us."

Franz Kafka

"I enjoy reading biographies because I want to know about the people who messed up the world."

Marie Dressler

"All my good reading, you might say, was done in the toilet."

Henry Miller

"I'm the kind of writer people think other people are reading."

V. S. Naipaul

"Be careful about reading health books. You may die of a misprint."

Mark Twain

"I have given up reading books. I find it takes my mind off myself."

Oscar Levant

"In the end all books are written for your friends."

Gabriel Garcia Marquez

"One always tends to overpraise a long book because one has got through it."

E. M. Forster

"Where do I find the time for not reading so many books?"

Karl Kraus

"I never travel without my diary. One should always have something sensational to read in the train."

Oscar Wilde

FAR FROM THE MADDING CROWD
10 reclusive scribes

J. D. SALINGER
Retired into his shell shortly after the publication of *The Catcher in the Rye* and has stoically resisted anyone trying to break through it.

SAMUEL BECKETT
Even refused to come out of seclusion to accept the Nobel prize he won in 1969.

MARCEL PROUST
Was so devastated by the death of his mother when he was 35 that he retired totally from public life.

EMILY DICKINSON
From the age of 30 she never left home, seeing visitors only rarely and limiting most of her relationships to the epistolary level. She saw nobody outside her family for the last 25 years of her life. Only six of her poems were published in her lifetime, and none of these with her consent. The process of writing was therapy for her—she didn't need the added gratification of seeing her poems foisted upon the public. She wrote 1,775 altogether.

JOSEPH SHERIDAN LE FANU
Became inconsolable after the death of his wife and remained in seclusion in his Merrion Square residence in Dublin as a result. He also became preoccupied with death and the supernatural at this time, themes that were to become focal points in his writings thereafter. He did most of his writing in bed in the small hours, and was so seldom seen by his friends that they dubbed him "The Invisible Prince."

LEO TOLSTOY

Became a hermit toward the end of his life and gave away most of his material possessions.

NATHANIEL HAWTHORNE

Hawthorne's mother, who was widowed when he was 4, brought him up in almost total seclusion and it was a lifestyle he carried with him into adulthood. It wasn't, however, one that pleased him. As he said once in a letter to his friend Henry Wadsworth Longfellow, "I have locked myself in a dungeon and I can't find the key to get out."

B. TRAVEN

This was the pseudonym of Berick Traven Torsvan alias Ret Marut, a political activist among communists and anarchists in Weimar Germany. He fled to Mexico in the 1920s under mysterious circumstances, and disappeared from the public eye while continuing to produce a steady stream of novels including the classic *Treasure of the Sierra Madre*.

THOMAS PYNCHON

Chronicles late twentieth-century conspiracy and paranoia in his novels and attempts to stay away from the media carousel. There is only one known photograph of him.

DON DELILLO

Even wrote a novel about a literary recluse (*Mao II*) and a rock-star recluse (*Great Jones Street*). He temporarily came out of hiding in 1998 to promote his *magnum opus Underworld*.

DON'T CALL US
10 best-selling books originally rejected

Dubliners James Joyce
Rejected by twenty-two publishers. When it was eventually published in 1922, it was ritually burned in the streets of Dublin for alleged obscenity. Would never have made it onto the shelves without the generous cash injections of Joyce's sponsor Harriet Shaw Weaver.

M*A*S*H Richard Hooker
Rejected by twenty-one publishers before it became a smash both on the bookshelves and on movie theater and TV screens.

Jonathan Livingstone Seagull Richard Bach
A total of eighteen publishers turned it down before Macmillan accepted. It flew off the shelves, became a Book-of-the-Month selection in 1972, and was then sold to Avon for $1 million for the paperback edition. By 1975, more than seven million copies had been sold in the U.S.A. alone.

Lorna Doone R. D. Blackmore
Rejected by eighteen publishers, it even flopped at its first print-ing in 1869. Two years later, however, it took off, and became a number-one bestseller in 1874. It has remained in print ever since, and three movie versions have been made.

Lust for Life Irving Stone
This novel about Vincent van Gogh was rejected by seventeen publishers but has now sold more than 30 million copies. It was also made into a 1956 movie version, with Kirk Douglas winning an Oscar nomination for playing the tortured painter.

Dune Frank Herbert
Herbert's sci-fi tale was declined by thirteen publishers for being too obvious and long-winded before it earned both critical and commercial raves in the 1960s.

The Ginger Man J. P. Donleavy
Rejected by numerous publishers in Ireland and the U.S.A. before Mr. Donleavy, on Brendan Behan's advice, decided to submit it to the controversial Olympia press in Paris. It subsequently became a sensation, but success may have spoiled Donleavy as he's published little of note since: his subsequent literary endeavors have been characterized by a kind of machismo that seems at odds with his verbose overtones.

Animal Farm George Orwell
Rejected by a number of publishers despite Orwell's reputation, which was well established when he wrote it. Victor Gollancz, Jonathan Cape, and Faber (where T. S. Eliot was at the helm) all turned it down. It was finally published by Warburg and proceeded to become a cult classic.

The Catcher in the Rye J. D. Salinger
Harcourt Brace amazingly didn't want this evergreen rite-of-passage classic before it was accepted by Little, Brown.

Lolita Vladimir Nabokov
Another future million-seller that was originally published by the Olympia press because of its controversial subject matter was too hot for other publishers to touch.

RETURNED TO SENDER

10 classics originally rejected for publication

Ulysses James Joyce
Pride and Prejudice Jane Austen
Lord of the Flies William Golding
Catch-22 Joseph Heller
Tess of the D'Urbervilles Thomas Hardy
The Wind in the Willows Kenneth Grahame
The Spy Who Came in from the Cold John Le Carré
The Rainbow D. H. Lawrence
The War of the Worlds H. G. Wells
Confederacy of Dunces John Kennedy Toole

In 1977, a cynical scribe submitted Jerzy Kosinski's 1969
National Book Award winner, *Steps*, to fourteen publishers and
thirteen literary agents as an unsolicited manuscript ... and all
said no to it. (Of course it can work the other way, too. I knew a
man at university who took a poem by e.e. cummings, wrote it
out back to front, and submitted it to a pretentious literary magazine.
It won first prize in the publication's competition for new talent.)

KEEP IT IN THE FAMILY
20 writer relations

MONICA DICKENS
Great-granddaughter of Charles Dickens

VIRGINIA WOOLF
Granddaughter of William Makepeace Thackeray

HENRY JAMES
Brother of author and philosopher William James

JOSEPH SHERIDAN LE FANU
Grandnephew of Richard Brindsley Sheridan

FRANCIS TROLLOPE
The mother of Anthony, and author of more than 115 books

MARGARET DRABBLE
Sister of A. S. Byatt

LAWRENCE DURRELL
Brother of the naturalist author Gerald Durrell

ALEXANDRE DUMAS
Both father (*père*) and son (*fils*), who shared the same name,
were hugely successful authors

MARTIN AMIS
Son of Kingsley, and if he continues at his accustomed rate, his
output threatens to emulate his father's

ANTHONY SHAFFER
This playwright (he wrote *Sleuth*) is the brother of Peter,
acclaimed author of *Equus*, among other works

PETER BENCHLEY
The *Jaws* author is the son of the humorist Robert Benchley

ALDOUS HUXLEY
Great-nephew of Matthew Arnold

COLIN MACINNES
Cousin of Rudyard Kipling

S. J. PERELMAN
Brother-in-law of Nathanael West

JOHN DRYDEN
Cousin of Jonathan Swift

PERCY BYSSHE SHELLEY
Son-in-law of novelist philosopher William Godwin

THOMAS MANN
Father-in-law of W. H. Auden

CHARLOTTE PERKINS GILMAN
Great-niece of Harriet Beecher Stowe

ADAM LIVELY
Son of Penelope Lively

MARY SHELLEY
Daughter of Mary Wollstonecraft Godwin

FOR GOD'S SAKE
10 writers on religion

"Religion consists in believing that everything that happens is extraordinarily important. It can never disappear from the world precisely for this reason."

Cesare Pavese

"To die for religion is easier than to live for it."

Jorge Luis Borges

"There is something wrong with a man if he doesn't want to break the Ten Commandments."

G. K. Chesterton

"After coming in contact with a religious person I always feel that I must wash my hands."

Friedrich Nietzsche

"To all things cleric/I am allergic."

Alexander Woollcott

"Religion has done love a great service by making it a sin."

Anatole France

"All religions are founded on the fear of the many and the cleverness of the few."

Stendhal

"We have just enough religion to make us hate, but not enough to make us love one another."

Jonathan Swift

"Pound notes are the best religion in the world."

Brendan Behan

"The basic problem for a writer is that if God exists, what is the point of literature? And if He doesn't exist, what is the point of literature?"

Eugene Ionesco

A CATHOLIC EDUCATION

5 converts to Rome

OSCAR WILDE
Converted to Catholicism the day before he died of cerebral meningitis in 1900.

PAUL VERLAINE
Underwent a conversion to Catholicism in 1873 when he was imprisoned for an attack on his poet-lover Arthur Rimbaud.

TENNESSEE WILLIAMS
Converted in 1968. His work suffered afterward.

JAMES BOSWELL
Ran away to London in 1760 and was secretly converted.

G. K. CHESTERTON
Converted in his late 40s and wrote the lives of both Francis of Assisi and Thomas Aquinas.

REVENGE IS SWEET

10 quotes on reviewers by the reviewed

"For critics I care the five hundred thousandth part of the tithe of a half-farthing."

Charles Lamb

"A good writer isn't *per se* a good critic anymore than a good drunk is automatically a good bartender."

Jim Bishop

"A great deal of contemporary criticism reads to me like a man saying, 'Of course I do not like green cheese; I am very fond of brown sherry.'"

G.K. Chesterton

"It's a short walk from the hallelujah to the hoot."

Vladimir Nabokov

"While an author is living, we estimate his powers by his worst performance, and when he is dead we rate him by his best."

Samuel Johnson

"The reviewer, reviewing my book/At which he had barely/Intended to look."

Hilaire Belloc

"I never read a book before reviewing it. It prejudices me so."

Sydney Smith

"One cannot review a bad book without showing off."

W. H. Auden

"There's only one thing to do with critics: bathe them in hot tar. If I listened to them I'd have been in the madhouse years ago."

Brendan Behan

"Unless the bastards have the courage to give you unqualified praise, I say ignore them."

John Steinbeck

CATCHERS IN THE WRY

10 writerly ripostes

Samuel Beckett was coming out of a café with a friend, who looked up at the clear-blue sky and said, "On a day like this, isn't it good to be alive?" Beckett thought for a moment and then said, "I wouldn't go quite as far as that!"

When a publisher was asked if he knew Michael Sadler's *Trollope,* he replied, "I'm afraid I haven't had that pleasure."

F. Scott Fitzgerald said to Ernest Hemingway, "The rich are different from you and I." Hemingway replied, "Yes, they have more money."

The poet Alfred Austin was complaining to Lord Young about his indigent circumstances, and said, "I manage to keep the wolf from the door." Young inquired, "How—by reading your poems to him?"

Alexandre Dumas was asked to contribute 25 francs to bury a bailiff. No great lover of such a breed, he whipped out 50 francs from his pocket and roared, "There you are—bury two of them!"

An actress in one of Coward's plays fluffed her lines during a rehearsal. "I knew them backwards last night," she said defiantly, which caused Coward to hit back with, "And that's exactly the way you're saying them this morning."

Oliver St. John Gogarty was once involved in a lawsuit with a fellow senator. Asked if he thought it would come to a battle of wits, he said, "No, I would never fight an unarmed man."

Lytton Strachey was a conscientious objector to war. During one cross-examination by the chairman of a military tribunal, he was asked, "Tell me, Mr. Strachey, what would you do if you saw a German soldier trying to violate your sister?" Strachey, who was gay, immediately retorted, "Get between them!"

Edna Ferber met Noel Coward at the Algonquin Hotel, dressed in a pant suit. He told her she almost looked like a man. "So do you," she replied.

Truman Capote was once approached by a man in a bar. The man took out his penis and asked Capote to autograph it. Capote looked long and hard at it, and replied, "Maybe I could initial it."

CALLS OF THE WILDE
10 ripostes from Oscar Wilde

Wilde once said to Max Beerbohm Tree, "I've always regarded you as the best critic of my plays." When Beerbohm Tree said that he couldn't ever remember criticizing Wilde's plays, Wilde replied, "That's precisely why, my dear fellow."

An admirer of his ran up to him in the street one day, but he didn't recognize her. "Oh but Mr. Wilde," she said, "don't you remember me? My name is Smith." "I remember your name perfectly," Wilde told her, "but I can never think of your face."

Wilde was once asked to name his one hundred favorite books but replied that he couldn't, "because I've only written five."

An enemy of Wilde's once said to him, "I passed your house last night." Wilde replied, "Thank you so much."

When asked once at a customs check if he had anything to declare, he replied famously, "Nothing except my genius."

During a bout of depression, a friend asked Wilde what was making him feel down. "I'm sad because one half of the world doesn't believe in God," he replied, "and the other half doesn't believe in me."

A man tried to cut him down to size one day by saying, "There goes that bloody fool Oscar Wilde." Wilde was unperturbed, however: "It's amazing," he said, "how soon one gets known in London."

When Arthur Balfour asked him what his religion was, he thought for a moment and then said, "I don't have any. I'm an Irish Protestant."

An acquaintance was boasting about his hectic social life and Wilde said to him, "I firmly believe you have dined in every house in London … once."

Sir Lewis Morris complained to him that there was a conspiracy of silence on the part of the press with regard to his literary output. "What ought I do, Oscar?" he asked. "Join it!" Wilde told him.

S

BEST-SELLERS

5 novelists with impressive sales figures
(The figures in brackets represent an aggregate for all their works)

Agatha Christie (2 billion)
Barbara Cartland (650 million)
Harold Robbins (250 million)
Jackie Collins (200 million)
Arthur Hailey (150 million)

The 10 top-selling books of all time

The Bible (3.88 billion)
Quotations from the Works of Mao Tse-Tung (800 million)
Noah Webster's *American Spelling Book* (100 million)
The Guinness Book of Records (90 million)
The McGuffey Readers (60 million)
Elbert Hubbard's *A Message to Garcia* (45 million)
World Almanac (40 million)
Benjamin Spock's *Common Sense Book of Baby and Child Care* (40 million)
Jacqueline Susann's *Valley of the Dolls* (30 million)
Margaret Mitchell's *Gone with the Wind* (30 million)

HAMMER AND TONGUES
10 classic examples of literary sarcasm

DENISE ROBINS
Once told Barbara Cartland she had written eighty-seven books. "That's nothing," Cartland replied, "I've written 145." "I see," said Robins, "One a year."

W. SOMERSET MAUGHAM
Was so underwhelmed with Spencer Tracy in the movie version of *Dr. Jekyll and Mr. Hyde* that he remarked at one point in the movie, "Which one is he playing now?"

DOROTHY PARKER
When a woman she didn't like said, "I can't bear fools," Parker replied, "Apparently your mother didn't have the same difficulty."

GORE VIDAL
After he heard that Truman Capote had died, remarked, "Good career move."

NOEL COWARD
When informed that an intellectually challenged actor had blown his brains out, he said, "He must have been an incredibly good shot."

R. B. SHERIDAN
When a servant of his dropped a tray, making an almighty din, Sheridan said, "I suppose you've broken all the plates." The servant said that he hadn't broken any at all, whereupon Sheridan commented, "Then you mean all that noise was for nothing?"

SAMUEL BECKETT

During his teaching days in Belfast the principal told him that his pupils were "the cream of Ulster." "Yes, rich, and thick!" he replied.

DAME EDITH EVANS

When informed that Nancy Mitford was staying at a friend's house to finish a book, she said, "Really? So what's she reading?"

EVELYN WAUGH

After his avowed enemy Randolph Churchill went into hospital to have a benign tumor removed, Waugh commented, "What a typical triumph of modern science to find the only part of Randolph that was not malignant and remove it."

PIA ZADORA

Alleged to have been so abysmal in a stage production of *The Diary of Anne Frank* that, when the Nazis arrived onstage looking for her, someone in the audience shouted out, "She's in the attic!"

TALES FROM THE SCRIPT

10 pieces of screenwriting trivia

In the Mary Pickford/Douglas Fairbanks version of *The Taming of the Shrew*, the credits read: "Screenplay by William Shakespeare, with additional dialogue by Sam Taylor."

Ben Hecht was even more corrosive. "I'm a Hollywood writer," he emoted, "so I put on my sports jacket and take off my brain."

Ernest Hemingway had this piece of rather direct advice for would-be screenwriters: "First of all you finish your book. Then you drive to where the California stateline is. Then you pitch your manuscript across. No. First let them toss the money over. Then you pitch it across. And then you get the hell out of there."

After Irwin Shaw saw the filmed version of his novel *The Young Lions,* he hardly recognized it, largely due to the character changes that Marlon Brando made. "Great movie!" he exclaimed. "Who wrote the book?"

On the first day of shooting *The Ipcress File*, director Sidney Furie put the script on the ground and set fire to it.

Frank Deferd gave this definition of screenwriters, as viewed by Hollywood: "First drafts of human beings."

When Raymond Chandler was asked who was the killer in *The Big Sleep*, he replied, "It's so confusing, I'm not even sure myself."

Kenneth Branagh won an Oscar for his 1996 *Hamlet* screenplay … even though he didn't change a word of Shakespeare's original.

Robert Towne was so disgusted with the manner in which the makers of *Greystoke* bowdlerized his script that he disowned it, giving the credit instead to P. H. Vasak … which happened to be his recently deceased Hungarian sheep dog.

Nelson Algren said that he was once offered a week's work in Hollywood as a screenwriter for £1,000. He worked Monday, got fired on Wednesday, and the man who employed him was out of town on Tuesday.

BUTCHERING MY BABY

15 writers who adapted another author's work for the screen

David Mamet, *The Postman Always Rings Twice* by James M. Cain
Edward Albee, *Lolita* by Vladimir Nabokov
Christopher Isherwood, *The Loved One* by Evelyn Waugh
Robert Bolt, *Dr. Zhivago* by Boris Pasternak
Harold Pinter, *The French Lieutenant's Woman* by John Fowles
Harold Pinter, *The Handmaid's Tale* by Margaret Atwood
Harold Pinter, *The Trial* by Franz Kafka
Raymond Chandler, *Double Indemnity* by James M. Cain
James Agee, *The Night of the Hunter* by Davis Grubb
Anthony Minghella, *The English Patient* by Michael Ondaatje
Terence Rattigan, *Goodbye Mr. Chips* by James Hilton
William Faulkner, *The Big Sleep* by Raymond Chandler
Frank McGuinness, *Dancing at Lughnasa* by Brian Friel
Aldous Huxley, *Jane Eyre* by Charlotte Brontë
Dalton Trumbo, *The Fixer* by Bernard Malamud

MOVIE MADNESS

5 unlikely screenwriting credits

On Her Majesty's Secret Service Anthony Burgess
King Kong Edgar Wallace
Yellow Submarine Erich Segal
You Only Live Twice Roald Dahl
Casino Royale Joseph Heller

IN ON THE ACT
5 male writers on sex

"To have a woman to lye with when one pleases, without running any risk of the cursed expense of bastards—that is the virtue of matrimony."

Robert Burns

"I can always find plenty of women to sleep with, but the kind of woman that is really hard for me to find is a typist who can read my writing."

Thomas Wolfe

"All a writer has to do to get a woman is say he's a writer. It's an aphrodisiac."

Saul Bellow

"A man marries to have a home, but also because he doesn't want to be bothered by sex and all that sort of thing."

W. Somerset Maugham

"Sex isn't even as important as excretion. A man can go seventy years without a piece of ass, but he can die in a week without a bowel movement."

Charles Bukowski

THE OLDER THE FIDDLE
10 authors who enjoyed an active sex life in later years

H. G. WELLS
Sexually active until his late 70s.

HENRIK IBSEN
Had an affair with the 27-year-old Hildur Anderson when he was 63.

VICTOR HUGO

Continued to have sex until his death at the age of 83. In his 70s, he had an affair with the actress Sarah Bernhardt, who was fifty years his junior, as well as a 27-year-old laundress.

HAVELOCK ELLIS

A late beginner in the boudoir, he was impotent until the age of 60. He made up for lost time thereafter and remained sexually active until he was 72.

BERTRAND RUSSELL

Was having affairs until his late 70s, and married for the fourth time at the ripe age of 80 in 1952.

W. SOMERSET MAUGHAM

The bisexual Maugham had an affair with his male secretary Alan Searle at the age of 72. (Searle was only 41 at the time.)

W. B. YEATS

Sex in his later years, he claimed, goaded him into further literary creativity. "What else have I to spur me into song?" he asked.

COLETTE

Was 52 when she married her third husband Maurice Goudeket. She claimed that this marriage was the most passionate.

JOHANN GOETHE

Was sexually active into his 70s, actually proposing marriage to a woman when he was 74.

MARQUIS DE SADE

At the age of 72 took the 25-year-old Madeleine Leclerc as his mistress.

HIDEOUS KINKY
5 writers who were sexually abused

CARL JUNG
Abused as a child by a man he said he worshiped—which led to a deep interest in some of the concerns that his friend Sigmund Freud was exploring in his work.

EMILE ZOLA
Abused at the age of 7 by one of his servants.

VIRGINIA WOOLF
Sporadically abused from the age of 6 to 22 by her two half-brothers, Gerald and George Duckworth. It started the day Gerald lifted her up onto a table and proceeded to explore her private parts; fifty-three years later she confessed to a friend, "I still shiver with shame at the memory of it all."

ANAÏS NIN
Was repeatedly fondled by her father between the ages of 9 and 11, and they came close to having sex. He later begged her not to put such memories in her diary, but she did.

LORD BYRON
His family nurse fondled him sexually when he was only 9, as well as allowing him to watch her make love to her many suitors.

THE TAMING OF THE SHREW
10 sexist remarks from authors

NORMAN MAILER
In a speech in Berkeley, California, in 1972, he made a comment that hardly endeared him to the women's liberation movement: "A little bit of rape is good for a man's soul."

SAMUEL JOHNSON
Remarked in 1763, "A woman's preaching is like a dog walking on his hindlegs. It is not done well, but you are surprised to find it done at all."

LEO TOLSTOY
Once said: "So-called decent women differ from whores mainly in that whores are less dishonest."

G. K. CHESTERTON
In his book *Women,* he wrote, "There are only three things in the world that women do not understand: Liberty, equality, and fraternity."

HENRY MILLER
In an interview in 1975, he said that he enjoyed women "as a breed, like a dog. They're another species that you become endeared to, like a fine breed of horse."

CONFUCIUS
Wrote in 500 B.C.: "Such is the stupidity of woman's character, it is incumbent upon her, in every particular, to distrust herself and to obey her husband."

W. H. AUDEN
Said of women, "When people are talking they should retire to the kitchen."

D. H. LAWRENCE
Once told Katherine Mansfield, "A woman must yield precedence to a man. Men must go ahead and women must follow them unquestioningly."

HONORÉ DE BALZAC
"A woman is a well-served table," he once said, "that one sees with different eyes before and after the meal."

NOEL COWARD
Said facetiously that women should be struck regularly "like gongs."

WHATEVER TURNS YOU ON
10 sexual eccentricities, fetishes, and perversions

YUKIO MISHIMA
Was sexually stimulated by sweat and male armpit hair.

VICTOR HUGO
Was a foot fetishist—as were F. Scott Fitzgerald and Fyodor Dostoevski.

JAMES BOSWELL
We know from his journals that he liked having sex in public places while standing up.

JAMES JOYCE
Was turned on by Nora's unwashed underwear: "that little brown stain on the seat of your white drawers". He even carried a pair of panties round with him in his pocket, to be taken out and caressed at will.

ERNEST HEMINGWAY
Believed that we have only a limited number of orgasms allotted to us in life and we can't go beyond that tally.

ALGERNON CHARLES SWINBURNE
Once had sexual relations with a monkey, which he dressed up as a woman. When it became jealous of one of his human friends and tried to bite him, Swinburne had it grilled and served for lunch. Another time, he confessed to Turgenev that he had a fantasy about deflowering a saint while she was in the ardent ecstasy of prayer—but with her secret consent.

JEAN-JACQUES ROUSSEAU
Liked to hide in dark alleys and expose himself to passing females.

HONORÉ DE BALZAC
Believed that sex drained his creative juices. Once when he was leaving a brothel he bade farewell to the lady who had serviced him with the immortal words, "There goes another novel!"

GABRIELLE D'ANNUNZIO
Tried to make a nun fondle his genitals, at the age of 12.

HAVELOCK ELLIS
Liked to watch women urinating, and once persuaded his lover Françoise Cyon to do so in Oxford Circus in front of a crowd of people.

WHERE THERE'S A WILL

10 Shakespearean oddities

There were no actresses allowed onstage in his time, which meant that female parts had to be played by men.

He had eleven different ways of spelling his name.

The phrase "Right on" appears in Act 3 Scene 2 of *Julius Caesar*.

The Comedy of Errors is the only one of his plays that doesn't have a song in it.

There are only seven known specimens of his signature in existence.

John Dryden's brother-in-law rewrote *Romeo and Juliet*, with an ending in which the eponymous characters lived happily ever after.

He only mentions America once in all his plays: in Act 3 Scene 2 of *The Comedy of Errors*.

Samuel Johnson once claimed that Shakespeare couldn't write six consecutive lines without a fault in them.

He was the first writer to use the words "bog," "bump," "assassination," "hurry," "lovely," and "dwindle."

There have been more than 400 movies made of his plays.

IN A BARD WAY
10 authors alleged to have written Shakespeare's plays

Edmund Spenser
Sir Philip Sidney
Anne Hathaway
John Donne
Cardinal Thomas Wolsey
Francis Bacon
Christopher Marlowe
Ben Jonson
Sir Walter Raleigh
Daniel Defoe

THE MERCHANT OF MENACE
10 Shakespearean insults

"He hath been five thousand year a boy."
"All that is within him does condemn itself for being there."
"It is certain that when he makes water, his urine is congeal'd ice."
"His wit's as thick as Tewksbury mustard."
"O tiger's heart wrapp'd in a woman's hide!"
"Thy food is such as hath been belch'd on by infected lungs."
"Would thou wert clean enough to spit upon!"
"I'll beat thee—but I should infect my hands."
"You whoreson cullionly barbermonger!"
"I hade rather be married to a death's head with a bone in his mouth."

ALL THE WORLD'S A STAGE

5 lines from Shakespeare now in common usage

"Neither a borrower, nor a lender be" *Hamlet*
"Making the beast with two backs" *Othello*
"Brevity is the soul of wit" *Hamlet*
"All that glisters is not gold" *The Merchant of Venice*
"Shuffle off this mortal coil" *Hamlet*

LOVE'S LABOR LOST

5 bad reviews of Shakespearean productions

"The best thing about Ian McKellen's *Hamlet* is his curtain call."
(Harold Hobson in 1971)

"Miss Bankhead played the Queen of the Nil."
(George Jean Nathan on Tallulah Bankhead's Cleopatra in
Antony and Cleopatra)

"Claire Bloom played Viola like a wistful little Peter Pan who is
worried to death about Tinkerbell." (*Time and Tide*, 1953)

"He looked like a coalminer with a tail coming up from the coal
face." (*Sunday Express* review of Richard Burton as Caliban in
The Tempest in 1954)

"Mr. Olivier plays Romeo as if he were riding a motorbike."
(Review of Laurence Olivier in a 1935 production of *Romeo and
Juliet* in London)

SHAW THINGS

10 examples of Shavian wit and repartee

When an actress wrote to him to say that she was "crazy to play St. Joan" in the play of that name, he wrote back to her saying, "I agree."

After his play *Candida* had a successful run on Broadway in 1935, he wrote a telegram to the actress Cornelia Otis Skinner saying, "Excellent! Greatest!" She cabled back, "A million thanks, but undeserving such praise." Shaw replied, "I meant the play," and Skinner, second-guessing the great man for once, had the last word with "So did I!"

He once asked a lady of dubious virtue if she'd sleep with him for £1,000, and she said she'd consider it. He then asked her if she'd do so for £100 and she said, "What do you think I am?" "We've already established that," said Shaw. "We're merely haggling about the price."

A heckler at a performance of one of his plays (which was enjoying fine reviews from other quarters) drew this response from the great man: "I agree with you, sir. But who are we among so many?"

When military theorist B. H. Liddell Hart told him that "sumac" and "sugar" were the only two words in English that had a "sh" sound with the "h" not being written, Shaw replied, "Sure".

Isadora Duncan was discussing the transmission of genes to children with him, and said to him, "Imagine a child with my body and your brain." Shaw shot back, "That would be nice, but what would we do if it had my body and your brain?"

He was listening to a string quartet one night but wasn't very impressed by the performance. On being informed that they had been playing together for twelve years, he said, "Surely we've been here longer than that."

He was listening to an orchestra on another occasion and, after finishing a piece, the leader asked him what he would like them to play next. "Dominoes," he advised.

Clare Boothe Luce, acknowledging his great influence on her career, said to him once, "If it wasn't for you I wouldn't be here." Shaw thought for a moment and then said, "Really? What was your mother's name?"

A woman wishing to meet him sent him a letter saying that she would be at home all day on a certain date. Shaw wrote back to her with the words, "So will I."

GET SHORTY
5 vertically challenged writers

Yukio Mishima (5'2")
Charlotte Brontë (4'9")
Samuel Pepys (5'1")
Alexander Pope (4'6")
Jean-Paul Sartre (4'6")

YEARS IN THE MAKING
5 slow scribes

ROBERT AINSWORTH
Began his famous *Latin–English Dictionary* in 1714, but didn't finish it until twenty-two years later. This was partly due to his bad eyesight, advancing age … and the fact that his wife threw a large chunk of it into the fire one day after an argument with him.

JAMES JOYCE
Took seventeen years to complete *Finnegan's Wake* (and nine for *Ulysses*).

PETER MARK ROGET
It took Roget, the author of *Roget's Thesaurus*, fifty years to finish his famous book, because he worked as a doctor by day during its composition.

GUSTAVE FLAUBERT
Spent eighteen years writing *Madame Bovary*.

KATHERINE ANNE PORTER
It took her over twenty years to complete her only novel, *Ship of Fools*.

WRITE AWAY
15 speedy scribes

EARLE STANLEY GARDNER
Dictated *The Case of the Velvet Claws* in three and a half days while holding down a law practice at the same time.

ANTON CHEKHOV
Wrote his one-act play *Swan Song* in one hour flat.

JAMES HILTON
Only took four days to write *Goodbye Mr. Chips*.

GEORGES SIMENON
Often claimed to have written eighty pages before breakfast, which represented four hours of dawn labor. He wrote more than 400 novels, as well as 1,000 stories and fifteen volumes of autobiography. He produced approximately one Maigret novel a month during the peak of his productivity. He once wrote a full novel in just twenty-five hours. His first book, *Au Pont des Arches*, was completed in ten days.

ROBERT LOUIS STEVENSON
Wrote *Dr. Jekyll and Mr. Hyde* in just three days—thanks largely to a nightmare he had, which (he claimed) presented him with the entire plot.

NOEL COWARD
Wrote *Private Lives* in a fortnight.

GORE VIDAL
Only took a week to churn out his early Edgar Box books; each of which contained seven chapters of 1,000 words each. He would do one chapter a day and then edit on the eighth day. (The month he spent writing *Myra Breckinridge*, by comparison, was positively snail-like.)

HILAIRE BELLOC
Wrote a biography of James II in eight days.

EDGAR WALLACE
Averaged six books a year, and once wrote one containing 80,000 words during a weekend.

JEAN COCTEAU
Wrote *Les Enfants Terribles* within three weeks.

ANNE RICE
Completed *The Interview with the Vampire* in five weeks to meet a deadline for a competition she was entering. She didn't win the competition, but the public liked it enough to make it a bestseller.

H. RIDER HAGGARD
Did *King Solomon's Mines* in just six weeks as the result of a boast he made to his brother that he could write an adventure as good as *Treasure Island*.

SIR WALTER SCOTT
Wrote fourteen novels within the space of six years at one point in his career.

JOHN CREASEY
Wrote 565 books in forty years, twenty-six of which were written in 1937. His average was twelve days for a book, but he once wrote two of them in half that time.

BARBARA CARTLAND
Equalled Creasey's record by writing 26 books in 1983.

FAST BUCKS
5 authors who wrote at speed for financial reasons

LOUISA MAY ALCOTT
Wrote *Little Women* in three weeks because she was her family's main source of income, and the recent death of her brother-in-law meant that her sister had a crisis on her hands.

SIR WALTER SCOTT
Wrote *Guy Mannering* in six weeks in order to pay off mounting debts on his bookselling business.

HONORÉ DE BALZAC
Wrote *Le Père Goriot* in forty days to pay off his debts, keeping himself going with endless cups of black coffee and working round the clock.

SAMUEL JOHNSON
Wrote *The History of Rasselas, Prince of Abyssinia* in a week in order to pay his mother's funeral expenses.

MARGARET OLIPHANT
Author of more than 100 books, as an early widower Oliphant wrote for her income and supported both her own and her brothers' families.

A BAD SPELL
5 writers who were bad spellers

Hans Christian Andersen
Aubrey Beardsley
Charles Dickens
Charles Bukowski
John Keats

THE CONFIDENTIAL AGENT

15 writers who were spies

BASIL BUNTING
Employed by MI6 to spy on Iran before his expulsion from that country in 1951.

GEOFFREY CHAUCER
Worked for the Crown in a top-secret capacity in the 1360s.

IAN FLEMING
Naval intelligence agent during World War II, covering trials of British spies for Reuters and also seizing German code books and equipment as troops began to invade France.

JOHN LE CARRÉ
Did national service in the Intelligence Corps in Australia.

CHRISTOPHER MARLOWE
Employed by the Secretary of State of Queen Elizabeth I to uncover Catholic plots against her.

APHRA BEHN
Spied for Charles II in Antwerp during the Dutch War.

ERSKINE CHILDERS
Employed in naval reconnaissance during World War II.

GRAHAM GREENE
Worked alongside Kim Philby before the latter's defection, and also spent time intercepting wireless messages.

EDMUND SPENSER
Carried dispatches from France and also wrote propaganda about Ireland.

JOHN MILTON
Latin Secretary to Oliver Cromwell's Party Council.

DANIEL DEFOE
Served under Queen Anne's government compiling secret dossiers on the party affiliations of VIPs, using the disguise of traveling salesman to do so (and to gather material for his books at the same time). When Queen Anne was replaced by George I, he continued to live his double life.

LORD BYRON
Was a member of the Carbonari secret society, which was dedicated to overthrowing foreign governments.

ANDREW MARVELL
Identified as a spy working for the Dutch in 1674 under the code name "Mr. Thomas."

ALEXANDRE DUMAS
Was a secret agent during the 1830 revolution in France.

W. SOMERSET MAUGHAM
British Intelligence sent him to Russia in 1917 disguised as a reporter working for U.S. publications, whereas his real purpose was to bring money to the Mensheviks and to carry messages home, thus retaining Russia as an active ally in World War I. He felt that he was the wrong man for the job due to his bad health, and afterward regretted his inability to prevent the Bolshevik takeover in Russia, and Russian withdrawal from the war.

THE FLASHING BLADE
5 literary stabbings

MARY LAMB
Having stabbed her mother to death and spent time in an asylum as a result, she cowrote *Tales from Shakespeare* with her brother Charles.

NORMAN MAILER
Stabbed his wife in 1960 after a quarrel. The wound was three inches deep and dangerously close to her heart, but she didn't bring charges against him and he walked free from court a year later.

SAMUEL BECKETT
Was once stabbed by a pimp in Paris, but showed more concern over the damage done to his coat than his physical injuries. His hospital bed was paid for by James Joyce.

DASHIELL HAMMETT
Had a large knife scar on his leg, an injury from his days as a Pinkerton detective.

CHRISTOPHER MARLOWE
Stabbed in the eye and killed at 29 during a brawl in a bar.

UNITED WE STAND
10 authors who liked to write standing up

Lewis Carroll
Benjamin Disraeli
Ernest Hemingway

Thomas Jefferson
Malcolm Lowry
Vladimir Nabokov
William Saroyan
Thomas Wolfe
Virginia Woolf
Sir Kenneth Clark

A SLIGHT IMPEDIMENT
5 writers who had problem stutters

W. Somerset Maugham
Lewis Carroll
Arnold Bennett
Charles Lamb
Elizabeth Bowen

HIGH NOTES
15 substance (ab)users

EDGAR ALLAN POE
Was addicted to alcohol and laudanum, which he used in order
to try to overcome the chronic depressions that assailed him.
(They only succeeded in exacerbating them.)

THOMAS DE QUINCEY
An opium addict. He started taking it for toothache, but eventually graduated to 10,000 drops a day. He experienced initial euphoria with it, but later became terrified of the nightmares that it brought in its wake.

SAMUEL TAYLOR COLERIDGE
Drank two quarts of laudanum a week, as well as amounts of Indian hemp. He said he composed *Kubla Khan* from an opium-induced sleep.

TENNESSEE WILLIAMS
Couldn't write without swilling wine.

ALEISTER CROWLEY
Was a daily user of heroin.

WILLIAM S. BURROUGHS
His life was one long experiment with drugs, but primarily morphine and heroin. His addiction is recounted in his first book *Junky*, originally published under the pseudonym, "William Lee."

VOLTAIRE
Was known to drink as many as fifty cups of tea per day, supplemented by another twenty of coffee.

SIGMUND FREUD
Smoked twenty cigars a day, even after being diagnosed as having cancer. Concerned that close readers of his work might see the habit as signifying some kind of phallic symbol, he said, "Sometimes a cigar is just a cigar." He also occasionally took cocaine to ease the pain of sinusitis, a condition that bothered him intermittently throughout his life.

CHARLES BAUDELAIRE
Was addicted to alcohol, opium, and hashish.

AUGUST STRINDBERG
Started taking morphine to help him sleep, but later it became a more general indulgence.

WILKIE COLLINS
Helped himself to ample doses of laudanum daily, as well as injecting himself with morphine. He also inhaled amyl nitrate, but this was for a medical condition. (He suffered from angina.)

ROBERT LOUIS STEVENSON
Was hooked on cocaine. Indeed, its mind-altering properties helped him to empathize better with his character(s) from *Dr. Jekyll and Mr. Hyde*, a novel he wrote mainly under the influence of the drug.

MARK TWAIN
Smoked more than forty cigars a day. "Giving up smoking is easy," he once said. "I've done it hundreds of times."

SAMUEL PEPYS
When he was 22 he was operated on for a bladder stone as big as a tennis ball. The operation made him pass what he called "gravel" in his urine, a condition that he tried to cure by drinking neat turpentine.

GRAHAM GREENE
Needed to complete *The Confidential Agent* in a hurry, so he took benzedrine—and then became hooked on it. (The book took him just six weeks to complete, as opposed to his customary nine months, thanks to the chemical boost.)

THE POWER AND THE GLORY
10 writers on success

"Success and failure are both difficult to endure. Along with success come drugs, divorce, fornication, bullying, travel, meditation, medication, depression, neurosis and suicide. With failure comes failure."

Joseph Heller

"It took me fifteen years to discover I had no talent for writing, but I couldn't give it up because by that time I was too famous."

Robert Benchley

"I detest and despise success, yet I cannot do without it. I'm like a drug addict. If nobody talks about me for a couple of months I have withdrawal symptoms."

Eugene Ionesco

"A man's reach should far exceed his grasp."

Robert Browning

"Everything yields to success, even grammar."

Victor Hugo

"For a hundred that can bear adversity there is hardly one that can bear prosperity."

Thomas Carlyle

"All you need in this life is ignorance and confidence, and then success is sure."

Mark Twain

"Whenever a friend succeeds, a little something in me dies."

Gore Vidal

"Of all the enemies of literature, success is the most insidious."

Cyril Connolly

"Never having been able to succeed in the world, he took his revenge by speaking ill of it."

Voltaire

TO BE OR NOT TO BE...

10 writers who committed suicide

ANNE SEXTON

Killed herself in October 1974 suffering from postnatal depression following the birth of her second child. She had attempted suicide many times before, once describing her attraction to suicide as being "like a moth sucking on an electric light bulb."

THOMAS CHATTERTON

Killed himself at the age of 17 by mixing arsenic with water, because of depression over his financial circumstances.

ARTHUR KOESTLER

Made a suicide pact with his third wife Cynthia Jeffries in 1983 after being diagnosed as having a terminal illness. Their last days together are recorded in the jointly written *Stranger in the Square*. Koestler had been an advocate of euthanasia all his life and was suffering from both leukemia and Parkinson's disease. Cynthia, however, was a healthy 55 (he was 77) and there's a school of thought that claims he forced her into the pact.

VIRGINIA WOOLF

Walked into the River Ouse with stones in the pockets of her coat and drowned herself.

ERNEST HEMINGWAY
Depression, alcohol, and dearth of inspiration all conspired to make him take his own life in July 1961, just like his own papa had done thirty years before. (His brother, sister, and granddaughter also topped themselves.)

SYLVIA PLATH
Put her head in a gas oven in 1963 at the age of 30 after a lifetime of turmoil. Her novel *The Bell Jar*, published the same year under the pseudonym "Victoria Lucas," chronicles the struggle of a woman against thoughts of suicide. Robert Lowell likened her last works to "playing Russian roulette with six cartridges in the cylinder."

CESARE PAVESE
Killed himself in a Turin hotel in 1950 at the age of 42, having spent many years in pain over writing frustrations and unrequited love.

YUKIO MISHIMA
At the age of 45, in the samurai ritual of *seppuku* he disemboweled himself. He was subsequently beheaded with his own samurai sword by one of his disciples, who then committed suicide himself.

PRIMO LEVI
Threw himself down a staircase in Turin in 1987 at the age of 68. His memory of the horrors of Auschwitz, where he was sent during World War I, is thought to have been a possible reason.

JOHN KENNEDY TOOLE
Ended his life out of frustration at not being able to find a publisher for his book *A Confederacy of Dunces*—it won him a posthumous Pulitzer Prize in 1981.

BACK FROM THE BRINK
10 writers who *attempted* suicide

GRAHAM GREENE
Put two dozen aspirin in a half-pint glass of whiskey as a young man when he was suffering from one of his familiar bouts of depression. He imagined that it would be a fatal concoction, but the aspirin neutralized the effect of the whiskey and vice versa.

JOHN KEATS
Tried to kill himself several times with overdoses of laudanum. He was suffering from depression and terminally ill with tuberculosis.

GUY DE MAUPASSANT
He tried to cut his throat in 1892 because he believed, during a manic phase, that his brain was seeping out through his nostrils.

ERNEST HEMINGWAY
Made many half-baked attempts to do himself in before he succeeded, walking out under the blades of a helicopter in one attempt.

F. SCOTT FITZGERALD
Once tried to kill himself by taking an overdose of morphine, but threw it all up.

CARSON MCCULLERS
Tried to kill herself due to depression over poor health, a barrage of strokes having confined her to a wheelchair in 1947. She recovered, but her husband afterward became obsessed with the idea of them both engaging in a suicide pact. She left him in fear of her life, and he did kill himself subsequently.

EDGAR ALLAN POE

Made a stab at ending it all by overdosing on laudanum in 1848, but he lived to tell the tale. (He was suffering from depression over his wife's recent death and his own out-of-control drink problem.) He actually took a full ounce of laudanum, which his stomach instantly rejected. Some of his biographers imagine that he knew enough about the substance to realize that this would happen, which made his act more a cry for help than a genuine suicide attempt.

DANTE GABRIEL ROSSETTI

Took an overdose of laudanum in 1872 after suffering a nervous breakdown.

CHARLES BAUDELAIRE

Worries about love, money, and his writing caused him to try and end it all at the age of 26. The would-be suicide note sounded convincing: "I am killing myself because I find the tedium of going to sleep and the tedium of waking up intolerable. I am killing myself because I am useless to others and a danger to myself."

WILLIAM COWPER

Tried to kill himself at least half a dozen times, having heard voices exhorting him to emulate the sacrificial act of Abraham with his son Isaac.

A LIFE LESS ORDINARY
5 odd facts about Jonathan Swift

Claimed that he only laughed twice in his whole life. On both occasions he was alone.

Once wrote a treatise on excrement, entitled *Human Ordure*, under the pen name "Dr. Shit."

Was such a fanatic for exercise that when it was raining he ran up and down the stairs of his house for hours on end.

Once refused to speak to anyone for an entire year.

Wrote a satirical treatise entitled *A Modest Proposal*, in which he suggested that Irish children, who provided "delicious, nourishing and wholesome food," should be stewed and roasted for the delectation of British stomachs.

T

EUNUCHS IN THE HAREM

10 views on theater critics

"Critics never worry me unless they're right—but that does not occur very often."

Noel Coward

"At any London night you'll see the critics creeping off to the pub halfway through Act III. Of course they pretend they have to catch the early editions."

Basil Boothroyd

"Critics should be searched for certain adjectives at the door of the theatre. I would have all such adjectives left with their coats in the foyer, only to be redeemed when their notices are written."

Alan Bennett

"One of the first and most important things for a critic to learn is how to sleep undetected in the theater."

William Archer

"Critics are like eunuchs in a harem. They're there every night, they see it done, they know how it should be done, but they can't do it."

Brendan Behan

"If Attila the Hun were alive today, he'd be a drama critic."

Edward Albee

"A drama critic is a man who leaves no turn unstoned."

George Bernard Shaw

"Critics: those who would send Hedda Gabler to the Marriage Guidance Council."

John Osborne

"It seems to me that giving Clive Barnes his CBE for services to the theater is like giving Goering the DFC for services to the RAF."

Alan Bennett

"Never pay attention to what the critics say: a statue has never been set up in honor of a critic."

Jean Sibelius

CATCALLS

5 examples of theatrical abuse

"He conducted the soul-selling transaction with the thoughtful dignity of a grocer selling a pound of cheese."

Hubert Griffith on Cedric Hardwicke in *Dr. Faustus* in 1948

"Wilfred Hyde-White prowls round the stage in search of laughs with all the blank single-mindedness of a tortoise on a lettuce hunt."

Criterion on White in *Not in the Book* in 1958

"It was as though someone had dramatized the cooking of a Sunday dinner."

Clement Scott reviewing *A Doll's House* in 1889

"Why must all the actors bellow like sea-lions conversing with walruses on the further side of an ice floe in a blizzard?"

James Agate on Paul Osborn's *A Bell for Adano* in 1945

"Hopkins was dressed like a cross between a fisherman and an SS man, evoking doggedly a Welsh rugby captain at odds with his supporters' club."

Clive James on Anthony Hopkins in *Coriolanus* at the Old Vic in 1971

ROSES BY ANOTHER NAME
25 original titles of famous books

Pride and Prejudice (First Impressions)
Alice in Wonderland (Alice's Adventures Underground)
War and Peace (All's Well That Ends Well)
Treasure Island (The Sea Cook)
The Time Machine (The Chronic Argonauts)
Jaws (The Summer of the Shark)
Portnoy's Complaint (A Jewish Patient Begins His Analysis)
Catch-22 (Catch-18)
Peyton Place (The Tree and the Blossom)
East of Eden (Salinas Valley)
Of Mice and Men (Something That Happened)
To Have and Have Not (The Various Arms)
Gone with the Wind (Ba Ba Black Sheep)
The Postman Always Rings Twice (Bar-B-Q)
Look Homeward, Angel (O Lost)
The Sound and the Fury (Twilight)
Lady Chatterley's Lover (Tenderness)
1984 (The Last Man in Europe)
The Great Gatsby (Incident at West Egg)
This Side of Paradise (The Romantic Egotist)
Portrait of the Artist as a Young Man (Stephen Hero)
Sons and Lovers (Paul Morel)
Sense and Sensibility (Elinor and Marianne)
Northanger Abbey (Susan)
She Stoops to Conquer (The Mistakes of a Night)

YOU HEARD IT HERE FIRST
10 origins of book titles

Gone with the Wind Margaret Mitchell
(*Non Sum Qualis Eram*, Ernest Dowson)

Tender is the Night F. Scott Fitzgerald
(Keats' 'Ode to a Nightingale')

Arms and the Man George Bernard Shaw
(Dryden's *Aeneid*)

Vanity Fair William Makepeace Thackeray
(Bunyan's *Pilgrim's Progress*)

The Grapes of Wrath John Steinbeck
(Julia Ward Howe's *The Battle Hymn of the Republic*)

From Here to Eternity James Jones
(Kipling's *Gentlemen Rankers*)

For Whom the Bell Tolls Ernest Hemingway
(John Donne's 'Devotions')

Of Mice and Men John Steinbeck
(Robert Burns' 'To a Mouse')

The Heart is a Lonely Hunter Carson McCullers
(William Sharpe's 'The Lonely Heart')

Of Human Bondage W. Somerset Maugham
(Spinoza's *Ethics*)

FIVE SHAKES OF A BOOK'S TAIL

5 famous book titles with Shakespearean origins

Brave New World Aldous Huxley (*The Tempest*)
The Dogs of War Frederick Forsyth (*Julius Caesar*)
Alms for Oblivion Simon Raven (*Troilus and Cressida*)
The Sound and the Fury William Faulkner (*Macbeth*)
Remembrance of Things Past Marcel Proust (*Sonnets*)

U

WRITE AND LEFT
10 unfinished and posthumously published novels

Adventures in the Skin Trade Dylan Thomas
Emma Charlotte Brontë
Felix Krull Franz Kafka
The Weir of Hermiston Robert Louis Stevenson
The Last Tycoon F. Scott Fitzgerald
The Garden of Eden Ernest Hemingway
The Mystery of Edwin Drood Charles Dickens
A Death in the Family James Agee
Billy Budd Herman Melville
The Man Without Qualities Robert Musil

ENDGAME
5 unfinished works that should have been lain to rest

True at First Light Ernest Hemingway (1999)
A substandard fictional memoir of a Kenyan safari, edited by his son. Papa left instructions that it was never to be published.

The Buccaneers Edith Wharton (1993)
A unfinished novel "reconstructed" by Marion Mainwaring from the author's synopsis.

Poodle Springs Raymond Chandler (1989)
Completed thirty-five years after his death by Robert B. Parker from a single first chapter.

The Siege of Malta Sir Walter Scott (1977)
Reconstruction from fragments of Scott's last novel written in
the aftermath of his stroke.

Iolani Wilkie Collins (1999)
A threadbare novel set in Tahiti, written when the author was
only 20.

V

BONFIRE OF THE VANITIES

10 writers who self-published

VIRGINIA WOOLF

Founded the Hogarth Press with her husband Leonard and published her first few books with it. The idea was that the manual labor of running a printing press would ease her psychological turmoil, but there was also a pragmatic benefit, as Leonard felt her writing was unlikely to be accepted by mainstream publishers before she became famous.

CHARLOTTE BRONTË

Published her first book of poetry privately. (It sold the grand total of two copies.)

RODDY DOYLE

Published his first book, *The Commitments*, under his own imprint of King Farouk Publishing. It went on to become a runaway success. Doyle later commented that the letter he wrote to the bank looking for a loan (and outlining his collateral) was a better work of fiction than the book itself.

J. M. BARRIE

Published his first novel, *Better Dead*, at his own expense in 1886. It cost him £25 in total, a not-inconsiderable sum at the time.

STEPHEN CRANE

Crane was unable to find a publisher for his first book, *Maggie: A Girl of the Streets*. It was rejected by every publisher he sent it to in 1839, so he borrowed some money from his brother and published it himself. It failed miserably, but two years later he had great success with *The Red Badge of Courage* and it was reissued, faring somewhat better the second time around.

BEATRIX POTTER
Published her first book, *The Tale of Peter Rabbit*, at her own expense in 1900, and also her second, *The Tailor of Gloucester*, in 1903.

WILLIAM BLAKE
Not only did he publish his own books, but he also made his own ink, hand-printed the pages—and got his wife to sew the covers on.

EDGAR WALLACE
Founded the Tallis Press in 1905 so that he could publish books of his that established publishers had repeatedly rejected.

JOHN GALSWORTHY
Self-published some early works under the pseudonym "John Sinjohn" before success came his way with *The Man of Property* in 1906.

MARCEL PROUST
Published *Remembrance of Things Past* in 1913 after it was rejected by a number of publishers.

PUBLISH AND BE DAMNED
10 fiction titles that made the Vatican index of forbidden books

Samuel Richardson's *Pamela*, 1744
Laurence Sterne's *A Sentimental Journey*, 1819
All Stendhal's love stories, 1840
Victor Hugo's *Les Misérables*, 1834–69
All George Sand's love stories, 1841–64

All Dumas' love stories, 1863
Flaubert's *Madame Bovary*, 1864
All D'Annunzio's love stories, 1911
Moravia's *The Woman of Rome*, 1952
Ernest Feydeau's *L'Hotel de Libre Echange*, 1864

15 writers in the Vatican index for their nonfiction

Thomas Hobbes
René Descartes
Francis Bacon
Montaigne
Baruch Spinoza
John Milton
John Locke
David Hume

Jean-Jacques Rousseau
Blaise Pascal
Oliver Goldsmith
Immanuel Kant
John Stuart Mill
Jean-Paul Sartre
Henri Bergson

ANIMAL WRITES
5 writers who were vegetarians

Leo Tolstoy
Percy Bysshe Shelley
James Boswell
George Bernard Shaw
John Keats

THEY DIED WONDERING

5 writers who were probably virgins all their lives

J. M. BARRIE
The author of *Peter Pan*.

HANS CHRISTIAN ANDERSEN
He had sensual feelings toward women but they weren't reciprocated. He sometimes visited brothels, but only to chat with the prostitutes. Some recent appraisals of his life speculate that he may have been a closet homosexual, and that *The Ugly Duckling* is actually a metaphorical parable about "coming out."

EMILY DICKINSON
Used poetry rather than people to release her undeniable sexual energy.

LEWIS CARROLL
Though he married the actress Mary Ansell, he never consummated the marriage and most likely died a virgin.

JOHN RUSKIN
His wife Euphemia Gray learned, to her chagrin, on their wedding night that he was unable to make love to her. The marriage was later annulled.

BAPTISMS OF FIRE

5 writers who lost their virginity to prostitutes

STENDHAL

The encounter resulted in him contracting syphilis, from which he suffered for the rest of his life.

GABRIELLE D'ANNUNZIO

Pawned his watch to pay for his baptism of fire with a Florentine lady of the night at the age of 16.

JAMES JOYCE

Lost his virginity at the tender age of 14 to one of the denizens of Dublin's red-light district "Monto", which figures as Nighttown in *Ulysses*. He was coming home from a play when he was waylaid.

H. G. WELLS

Lost his virginity to a prostitute at the age of 22, but had no other sexual experiences until the night of his honeymoon three years later. He had a rapacious sexual appetite in later life.

LEO TOLSTOY

Was 16 when the dreaded act occurred, and afterwards he sat at the foot of the woman's bed and cried.

W

A ROOM OF ONE'S OWN
Where they wrote: 5 authors' retreats

ROALD DAHL
Wrote all his books in a shed at the bottom of his backyard.

GEORGE BERNARD SHAW
Used a rotating work shed in his garden at Ayot St. Lawrence so he could get the best out of the sun.

P. G. WODEHOUSE
Typed his novels where he could not be disturbed—on a boat on the moat of his home, Hunstanton Hall in Norfolk.

STELLA GIBBONS
Allegedly wrote *Cold Comfort Farm* on her way to work every morning on the London Underground.

MARCEL PROUST
Worked in a soundproofed room with cork walls. He also bought up the neighboring apartments, keeping them empty in order to prevent noise.

Index